GIFTS
FROM THE
GARDEN

100 Gorgeous Homegrown Presents

GIFTS FROM THE GARDEN

100 Gorgeous Homegrown Presents

DEBORA ROBERTSON
PHOTOGRAPHY BY YUKI SUGIURA

KYLE BOOKS

AcKnowLEDGMenTs

First, I owe enormous gratitude to Kyle Cathie and everyone at Kyle Books for entrusting me with this lovely project. Huge thanks to Judith Hannam for steering me through the initial stages and Sophie Allen whose grace, patience, good humor, and razor-sharp mind made this book such a great pleasure to work on. With Helen Bratby, who designed these pages so beautifully, I felt in the safest and most creative of hands.

It is my great good fortune to have had the supremely talented Yuki Sugiura take the photographs for this book. Her enthusiasm for the project made shoot days a delight. And I am enormously indebted to my dear friend, stylist Tabitha Hawkins. I wish we could work together every day.

Thank you to my agent, Caroline Michel at PFD, for her enthusiasm, advice, and encouragement. I truly appreciate it.

And an #FF forever to gardening writer and Twitter pal Alex Mitchell, who first suggested I might like to talk to Kyle Books about this project.

Thank you to Nash Khandekar for all of his help and friendship over the years.

My weekly trips to Columbia Road Flower Market are made all the more enjoyable because of Carl, Mick, and Sylvia Grover. Their advice, wisdom, and friendship have enriched my garden and my Sundays for many years. Long may that continue.

Without my parents' endless patience with a small girl who loved to bake and make and generally leave a crafty mess in her wake, I would never have discovered the love of creating, cooking, and growing which continues to add untold pleasure to my daily life. If they're astonished that I somehow managed to spin that into a career, they have the good grace not to show it.

And finally, to my husband Séan, who is the greatest gift I ever gave myself: thank you for your tireless cheerleading, coffee making, clearing up, ferrying around, sampling, and suggesting. You're marvelous.

Kyle Books
Published in 2013 by Kyle Books
an imprint of Kyle Cathie Limited
www.kylebooks.com

Distributed by National Book Network
4501 Forbes Blvd., Suite 200
Lanham, MD 20706
Phone: (800) 462-6420
Fax: (301) 429-5746
custserv@nbnbooks.com

ISBN: 978-1-906868-92-5

10 9 8 7 6 5 4 3 2 1

Debora Robertson is hereby identified as the author of this work in accordance with section 77 of the Copyright, Designs and Patents Act 1988.

Design **Helen Bratby**
Photography **Yuki Sugiura**
Prop styling **Tabitha Hawkins**
Project and food styling **Debora Robertson**
Project editor **Sophie Allen**
Copy editor **Emily Hatchwell**
Proofreader **Ruth Baldwin**
Production **Gemma John and Lisa Pinnell**

Library of Congress Control Number: 2013931350

Color reproduction by Altaimage
Printed and bound in China by C&C Offset

CONTENTS

INTRODUCTION

Anyone who has ever grown lettuce in a window box or planted some bulbs in an old terra-cotta pot knows that the pleasure of growing something yourself often far exceeds the effort it takes. And by using the plants you grow to create gifts for those you love, you can prolong and share that pleasure and extend it even further.

Gardeners, like cooks, are generous people. You seldom leave the garden or kitchen of such a person without a cutting, a few seeds, a recipe, or a scrap of paper filled with hastily-scrawled tips. Transforming what you grow into gifts takes this instinct, packs it into a jar or box and wraps it all up in a pretty bow. Of course, your intention is to delight the recipient, but there is also a near-addictive enjoyment in creating such gifts too.

Making your own presents enhances your awareness of—and delight in—the passing seasons in unexpected ways. If you've rigged up a simple flower press at home, a country walk or a stroll around the garden is never the same again. You will always have an eye out for interesting leaves or grasses, perfect flowers, or seed heads. If you're making your own potpourri, every falling petal is no longer a source of sadness—it's an opportunity.

Some gifts, such as a batch of cookies, a jar of seasoned olives, or a simple bouquet, are the work of a few minutes. Others take a little more forward planning. Chutneys and liqueurs need to mature for a few weeks or months before you give them away. But there's something enormously satisfying in knowing that you have a stash of gifts ready to be packed up and given to friends and family.

For some of the gift ideas in this book, there's an initial investment in powders, potions, essential oils, and waxes, but a little goes a long way, and lasts a long time. You'll have them on hand next time you want to rustle up a quick bar of soap, face cream, or room spray. They'll also allow you to create unique gifts at a fraction of the cost of something mass-produced in a factory.

And there is an added benefit to making your own gifts. Not for you the anxiety-inducing dash through the mall, wearily checking off gifts from your present list with a resigned "That'll do." Making your own gifts allows you to give yourself permission to slow down and spend a few hours, a day or two, in activities which combine both playfulness and usefulness. The intrinsic pleasure in making your own presents means that you'll never have to battle with the crowds in a shopping center. You also have the comfort of knowing exactly what has gone into your jams, face masks, and polishes—there are no secret or sinister ingredients lurking beneath the pretty lids.

Deciding how to package your presents is almost as much fun as making them. Look out for old tins, pretty jars, lengths of ribbon, tags, stamps, and unusual papers and you can wrap them up in a fashion that would rival the attempts of the poshest boutiques.

We all know how much time and love goes into growing your own flowers, fruit, vegetables, and herbs. When we transform them into gifts, we're sharing more than a piece of our gardens, we're sharing a piece of our hearts. And there is nothing more generous than that.

STRAIGHT FROM THE GARDEN

While it's satisfying to create and give presents made from plants you've grown in your garden, sometimes the most touching gift of all is the simplest: a plant you've propagated and tended yourself. It's an inexpensive way of increasing your own stock as well as producing specimens which you can pot and give to friends.

There's nothing terribly difficult about dividing, layering, or taking cuttings to increase your plant supply, so even the most inexperienced of gardeners shouldn't feel daunted about giving it a try.

Taking cuttings

Take softwood cuttings in spring when the plant has plenty of healthy new shoots. Get everything ready before you start. You'll need a pruning knife, a 3in pot with drainage holes, filled with a mixture of potting soil and pea gravel, a watering can with a fine rose, a pencil or dibber, a length of strong wire, and a clear plastic bag.

Pull a nonflowering stem, about 4in long, from the plant with a small strip of bark, or "heel," attached. Trim the excess off the bark strip with a pruning knife. Use your knife to trim the lower leaves from the stem—you need only a few pairs of leaves to remain at the top and you need a decent length of bare stem to insert into the potting soil. Make four or five holes around the edge of the pot with a pencil or dibber and insert the prepared stems into them, firming them in gently with your fingers. Water in lightly.

Bend the wire into a loop that clears the tops of the cuttings by several inches. Insert the loop into the pot and place the plastic bag over the top, making sure it doesn't touch the leaves.

Put the cuttings in a warm, shaded place and remember to turn the bag inside out every few days to ensure the moisture doesn't drip down onto the leaves and make them wet, as this may cause them to rot. Once rooting is established and the cuttings start to show signs of new growth, snip the corner of the bag to increase circulation.

After 4–6 weeks, remove the bag completely, and when the cuttings start to look like healthy little plants, pot them up individually. Overwinter in a cold greenhouse or conservatory and plant the following spring.

SoME PLaNTs wHIch YoU cAn PRoPAGaTE BY

TAKING SOFTWOOD CUTTINGS Chamomile, lavender, lemon verbena, pelargoniums, pinks, rosemary, sage

LAYERING Bay, clematis, climbing roses, honeysuckle, pinks, sage, thyme

DIVIDING Bergamot, chamomile, chives, hardy geraniums, lemon balm, lemon grass, mint, pinks, thyme, wormwood

Dividing

Mint in pots or planted in the ground can die back in the center or become straggly after a while. Revive congested plants in spring by lifting them with a fork or carefully removing them from their pots. Use a fork, knife, or your hands to split the plant into separate pieces, each with their own root system. Replant in pots or in the ground and water

in well. When potting up plants, make sure the plant pots you use are scrupulously clean to avoid spreading diseases. Place some broken bits of terra-cotta pot in the bottom to help drainage and don't fill the pot right up to the brim with soil as this will make it difficult to water your plant later.

If you're using terra-cotta pots, while they look lovely, you may have a problem with them drying out during hot weather. To avoid this try lining the sides of the pot (don't block up the drainage holes) with plastic. I save empty potting soil bags and chop them up to line pots with—the tough plastic works very well and doesn't perish.

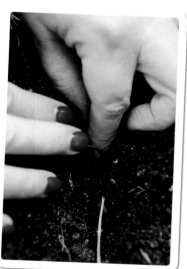

Layering

This is a very easy way to increase your supply of rosemary and is possibly the simplest propagation method of all.

In summer, choose a long, fresh, flexible, nonflowering stem about 10in long. Remove the rosemary leaves from all but the top 2in of the sprig and gently roughen the underside of your stem with a

pruning knife. This will encourage it to root.

Use a trowel or your fingers to make a thin trench, about 2in deep, adjacent to the mother plant. Place the prepared stem in the trench, ensuring that the leafy tip remains above the soil level. Make a pin of about 3in long with a piece of sturdy wire and use this

to anchor the stem in the ground. Cover the stem and trench with soil and water in well. Water little and often until the stem shows signs of new growth. In the fall, if the plant is well rooted, cut it away from its mother plant and pot. Alternatively, leave it in place until the spring before cutting it away and planting out in a new spot.

HERBS & FLOWERS

GRoWING bAY

Bay, *Laurus nobilis*, is an evergreen member of the laurel family, steeped in ancient folklore. Those handsome bay topiaries you often see outside fancy houses? It was believed that planting bay at entry points warded off witches, wizards, and lightning. Whether they ward off evil or not, they're enormously useful in the kitchen and not terribly demanding to grow. They're very happy grown in containers, which allows you to bring them inside when hard winter frosts threaten. Water sparingly during the winter and, if you're training your bay into a shape, prune it back in spring to help maintain its structure and promote fresh new growth. Bay trees do best when planted in well-drained soil in a sunny spot where they have some protection from harsh winds, though they will manage a little shade.

DEcoRATIvE InSPIRATIoN

SPRING: Auriculas, fragrant sprigs of *Osmanthus burkwoodii* or *Daphne odora*, variegated *Euonymous fortunei* leaves, ferns, pansies, flowering sprigs of rosemary

SUMMER: Achilleas, astrantias, campanulas, chiles, coneflowers, cornflowers, eryngiums, honeysuckle, some hydrangea blooms, irises, love-in-a-mist, marguerites, marigolds, sprigs of myrtle, pinks, scented pelargonium leaves and flowers, scabious, sunflowers, thrift flowers, roses, salvias, veronica

FALL: Any bright, autumn foliage such as cotinus, *Euonymus alatus*, ginkgo, liquidambar, oak leaves with acorns, maples, asters, Chinese lanterns, dahlias, fennel seed heads, dried honesty seed heads, poppy seed heads, pyracantha berries, rosehips, sorbus berries

Wrapping

A gift looks so much more charming and personal when it's attractively wrapped and embellished with simple cuttings from the garden. Unless you're wrapping and giving the present almost immediately, choose cuttings which will last for a while without wilting, such as evergreen sprigs of bay leaves and rosemary, fir cones, or small sprays of berries.

A wintery selection of bay leaves, berries, eucalyptus, fir cones, fir sprigs, holly, ivy, mistletoe, rosemary, dried orange and apple slices (see page 123)

Fine florist's wire
Pruning shears
Ribbon, garden twine, and/or raffia

This is hardly a "method," more an inspiration. Sprigs or sprays of foliage and herbs can simply be tucked under the ribbon on your package, but to make them more secure you can tie them in with wire that will then be hidden by the bow. If you'd like to carry the garden theme even further, garden twine and raffia come in many colors and provide an inexpensive, informal, and attractive alternative to ribbon.

If you like, berries and holly leaves can be frosted to give them a Christmassy/wintery appearance (see page 121). Fir cones can be sprayed gold, silver, or white, which looks particularly effective as an adornment to plain wrapping paper.

Decorated stationery

Pressed flowers, herbs, leaves, and seed heads are a great way to decorate gift tags, cards, boxes, and name cards for the dinner table, as well as making an original adornment to bought candles (see page 85).

A selection of dried flowers,
    seed heads, and/or leaves
A selection of paper
Clear craft glue
Tweezers

SOME GOOD THINGS TO PRESS

Wild chervil or Queen Anne's lace
Delphiniums
Ferns
Forget-me-nots
Single hydrangea blossoms
Larkspur
Pansies
Pinks
Poppies
Primrose
Individual rose petals
Verbena
Violets
Wormwood—flowers and leaves

Pick your specimens in peak condition and choose a dry day, after the morning dew has evaporated. Brush off any dust with a small, soft paintbrush and enclose the flowers in two sheets of watercolor paper. Either press them in a heavy book, weighed down beneath other heavy books, or use a flower press (see the box below). They're ready when they're completely dry and papery, which should take a couple of weeks. They're quite fragile, so handle them carefully— you might want to use tweezers.

If you're not using your flowers immediately, seal them in glassine bags and store them in a cardboard box in a cool, dry place.

Cut your papers into the size you want and fold them to make cards. Use a very thin layer of clear craft glue to stick the flowers onto the cards. Less is usually more—a single bloom, a perfect curl of fern, one beautiful leaf can look more elegant and effective than a more elaborate design.

TO MAKE SCENTED STATIONERY

If you're making a box of stationery as a gift, sew a simple muslin sachet (see Herbal Bathtime "Teas" on page 31) and fill it with dried, scented flower petals and herbs. Tuck the sachet into the gift box and after a week or so it will impart a subtle, sweet scent to the paper.

MAKING YoUR owN FLOWER PRESS

Of course you can buy a flower press, but often they're small and expensive. If you can drill a hole, they're easy to make yourself. You'll need two pieces of wood: about 12in square works quite well. In the four corners of each piece drill holes large enough for long bolts to be fitted through them. Cut out squares of cardboard and watercolor paper (available from good craft stores, art supply stores, and stationers) small enough to fit the area within the holes. Layer up the cardboard and watercolor paper, enclosing the flowers you want to dry between two sheets of watercolor paper. Place the bolts through the holes and secure tightly with wing nuts and washers.

Seed packets

You can be too tidy a gardener. While scrupulously deadheading plants can prolong flowering, it will deprive you of the pleasure of watching the often beautiful seed heads develop and of the thrifty satisfaction of collecting free seeds. As an added bonus, they make very good gifts for avid gardeners.

Pruning shears or scissors
Brown paper bags
Small glassine bags
Labels
Sewing machine or needle and thread

Allow seed heads to dry out as much as possible on the plant. Wait until the seeds look ripe—usually when they've turned brown or black—and choose a dry, still day to harvest them.

Cut off the seed heads, holding a bowl beneath the plant to capture any seeds which may fall as you work. For smaller flowers, such as pansies, it's enough simply to shake the seeds free from the flower heads into a bowl before bagging them up. For larger specimens, place the entire flower head in a paper bag, secure with an elastic band, label, and hang upside down in a dry place. When most of the seed pods have opened, tip the bag's contents out onto a pale surface and sort the seeds from any bits of the seed heads.

Put the seeds into the glassine bags and fold down the top. Type or write out seed labels, then secure them by sewing right across the bag. They make good gifts just as they are, but you can also turn them into pretty and unusual gift tags to tie onto presents by simply punching a hole into the seed bag above the sewn line and threading through string, ribbon, or raffia.

Stored in a cool, dry, airy place, seeds will remain viable for years, but germination is more reliable within a year or so.

SOME EASY SEEDS TO COLLECT

Aquilegia
Chives
Chinese lanterns
Foxgloves
Larkspur
Love-in-a-mist
Marigolds
Morning glory
Nasturtiums
Pansies
Poppies
Snapdragons
Sunflowers

Cook's window boxes

A themed window box, tailored to a friend's particular culinary passion, makes an original and thoughtful gift. And, the more you pluck at them, the better they grow.

Pizza window box

1 small arugula plant
1 small basil plant
1 small oregano plant
1 small chile plant
1 small cherry tomato plant

Thai window box

1 small lemongrass plant
1 small mint plant
1 small cilantro plant
1 small Thai basil (*Ocimum basilicum* horapa) and/or Holy basil (*O. sanctum*) plant
1 small chile plant

Fines herbes window box

1 small chervil plant
1 small tarragon plant
1 small parsley plant
1 small chives plant

Window box, or other suitable container
Broken crocks or pebbles
Potting soil
Slow-release fertilizer granules

If you're not using a window box, make sure that the container you're using has some drainage holes in the base. Add some broken crocks or pebbles to the bottom and fill with potting soil mixed with slow-release fertilizer granules, according to the instructions on the package. Plant up with the chosen herbs and water them in well.

A well-cared-for window box should last all summer.

GrowIng ARugula

Arugula, *Rucola coltivata*, is not only delicious scattered fresh over a just-out-of-the-oven pizza, but it's also great in fiery summer salads and can be ground into a sprightly pesto. It's very easy to grow from seed. Sow thinly directly into the ground or pot. It can run to seed quite quickly, so keep cutting at it and ensure it's well watered.

PACKAGING IDEA To make your planter an even more special gift, write out a card with care instructions for the herbs and tie it to the handle of some pruning shears or a watering can with a pretty ribbon, garden twine, or raffia.

Chive & lemon pesto

This is a sprightly, easy pesto to make when you're cutting back the first flush of growth from your chives before they flower. It's delicious on pasta or gnocchi, of course, but it's also very good as a dressing for just-boiled new potatoes. Makes approx. 1 x 7oz jar.

1/3 cup pine nuts
A generous bunch of chives,
    about 2 cups, finely chopped
2/3 cup Parmesan cheese, finely grated
Grated zest of 1 small lemon
1 small garlic clove, minced
4–6 tablespoons olive oil,
    plus a little more for bottling
Salt and pepper

1 x 7oz jar

Warm a dry frying pan over medium heat and gently toast the pine nuts until just golden and fragrant, rattling the pan frequently to ensure they do not burn. Cool and grind roughly in a mortar and pestle, or pulse a couple of times in a food processor. Combine with the chives, cheese, lemon zest, garlic, and just enough oil to get the texture you like. Taste and season if necessary with salt and pepper.

Spoon the pesto into the cold, sterilized jar, pressing down with the back of a spoon to get rid of any air pockets. Ensure that the pesto is completely covered by a thin layer of oil before sealing.

Refrigerated, the pesto will keep for 2–3 days.

GROWING CHIVES

Slender, grassy chives (*Allium schoenoprasum*) are one of the first herbs to poke their way through the soil to herald the beginning of spring. These clump-forming hardy perennials are very easy to grow and have so many uses in the kitchen, they earn their place in even the smallest of gardens. Keep them well watered in dry spells and trim them back quite close to the soil line before flowering to ensure lots of fine leaf growth. If you have room, do allow a clump or two to flower, though. The pretty purple pompoms which appear at the end of the leaves look and taste wonderful in salads.

PACKAGING IDEA To make a more substantial gift, combine this tangy pesto with a bag or two of beautiful fresh pasta and/or a mortar and pestle.

Both marjoram and oregano
are an invaluable addition
to the herb garden, with
marjoram having the slightly
milder, sweeter flavor that
makes it better added toward
the end of cooking time.
All of the following have
excellent flavor: Greek oregano
(*Origanum vulgare* subs.
hirtum), pot marjoram
(*O. onites*) and golden
marjoram (*O. vulgare*
'Aureum'). Trim the plants
after flowering to keep them
bushy and cut them back
to within about 2in of the
soil line in late fall.

Herbes de Provence

Making your own herbes de Provence allows you to adjust the balance of herbs until you have the flavor you like. Traditionally, this blend is a combination of herbs which grow wild in the hills of the South of France—the lavender is a more modern addition. Makes 1 x 5oz jar.

BASIC RECIPE

3 tablespoons dried thyme
2 tablespoons dried marjoram
1 tablespoon dried oregano
1 tablespoon dried summer savory
1 teaspoon dried rosemary
1 teaspoon dried lavender flowers
½ teaspoon fennel seeds
1 dried bay leaf

OTHER ADDITIONS YOU MAY LIKE

A little dried orange or lemon zest
Dried chervil
Dried tarragon
Dried mint
Dried basil
Dried dill

1 storage jar, about 5oz capacity

Combine the dried herbs in a mortar and pestle and crush roughly to blend. Seal in your chosen jar, which should be airtight.

This mixture is enormously versatile. It can be used as a dry spice rub for chicken or fish or combined with olive oil to make a marinade, scattered on potatoes before you roast them, sprinkled on pizza, or used to season stuffed tomatoes or in light, summery tomato sauces.

Sealed in an airtight container and stored in a cool, dark place, the herbes de Provence mixture will keep for up to 4 months.

Seasoned salts

Great for seasoning meat, fish, vegetables, and even sprinkling over popcorn, seasoned salts take just seconds to make. Use fresh herbs in the mixture as they have better flavor and will dry out in the salt, infusing it with their aromas. Pack the salts in clear glass jars and give them as a set—their striking colors make for a very attractive gift.

Chile salt

This salt adds a delicious kick of heat on everything from grilled sardines to steak or roasted potato wedges.

1/2 cup sea salt flakes
1 dried chile
1 teaspoon fresh oregano
1/2 teaspoon ground cumin
1/4 teaspoon smoked paprika

Thyme & orange salt

Very good sprinkled over roasted vegetables.

1/2 cup sea salt flakes
Finely grated zest of 1 small orange
2 tablespoons fresh thyme leaves and flowers

Citrus salt

Great on white fish, shrimp, and chicken.

1/2 cup sea salt flakes
Finely grated zest of 2 lemons
Finely grated zest of 1 lime

Dill salt

This salt works well sprinkled on salmon or roasted beets.

1/2 cup sea salt flakes
2 tablespoons fresh dill fronds
Finely grated zest of 1 small lemon
1/4 teaspoon freshly ground black pepper
A couple of pinches of dill seeds, if you have them

To make the seasoned salts, simply pulse the ingredients in a food processor until well blended or pound them together in a mortar and pestle. Store in airtight containers.

The salts will keep their flavors for a couple of months.

Bouquet garni

These little bundles of herbs impart great depth of flavor when added to slowly simmered soups, stews, and stocks. But the classic culinary trio of parsley, thyme, and bay leaves is really just the starting point. Include some tarragon for chicken or fish, a thinly pared strip of orange zest and some marjoram in bundles intended for beef casseroles, or rosemary to bring flavor to slow-cooked lamb dishes. Bouquet garni bundles make wonderful gifts for friends who are avid cooks.

THE ESSENTIAL COMBINATION
3 parsley stalks
2 thyme sprigs
1 bay leaf

Kitchen string
Labels
Jars

To go with chicken
A curl of lemon zest
Sprigs of tarragon
Fennel fronds

To go with beef
A curl of orange zest
Sprigs of marjoram and oregano

To go with pork
A curl of lemon zest
Sprigs of sage and myrtle

To go with lamb
Sprigs of rosemary, oregano,
  and marjoram

Simply tie together the bundles with string and hang them to dry in a dark, well-ventilated place before storing them in an airtight container. If you are making bundles to go with different kinds of dishes, don't forget to label them.

Stored in an airtight container, the bundles will keep their flavor for a month or so.

GROWING DILL
Dill, *Anethum graveolens*, is an annual herb that has an affinity with fish, potato, and egg dishes. Either start off the seed in plug trays (it doesn't like its roots disturbed), or sow it directly in the ground. In spring, once all threat of frost has passed, sow the seed thinly and cover with a fine layer of soil. Dill thrives in well-drained, fairly poor soil with a bit of shade. Once the seeds have established themselves, thin to about 10in apart and water well in hot spells to prevent the plants going to seed. Sow successive plantings over the summer to maintain a continuous supply. In fall, gather the seeds (see page 19).

COMPANION PLANTING PARSLEY
Parsley may be one of the most useful herbs in the kitchen, but its usefulness doesn't start there. It's a very good companion plant in the vegetable patch too. Allow some of your parsley to flower and it will attract predatory wasps to the garden which will devour harmful aphids. It's often planted alongside asparagus beds as it's thought to ward off asparagus beetle, and some believe that when planted among roses it intensifies their scent.

Seasoned spice rubs

Easy to make and a terrific way of adding instant flavor, spice rubs are great, simple gifts for avid cooks. Rub a fine sprinkling of the mixture into the meat about 30 minutes before cooking.

Myrtle spice rub

This blend is particularly good with venison, though it goes well with duck too.

Makes 1 x 2oz jar.

2 tablespoons fresh thyme leaves
2 tablespoons fennel seeds
2 tablespoons pink peppercorns
6 myrtle berries or juniper berries
2 cloves
2 tablespoons sea salt flakes
12 myrtle or bay leaves
½ teaspoon freshly grated nutmeg

1 small jar

With a mortar and pestle, pound together the thyme, fennel seeds, peppercorns, juniper or myrtle berries, and cloves, until you have a fairly coarse mixture. In a small bowl, stir in the mixture with the salt, mytle leaves, and nutmeg. Pour into a small jar and leave for a week for the flavors to blend. Be sure to remove the myrtle leaves before cooking as they can leave a bitter taste—you're simply infusing the rub with their flavor.

Coriander spice rub

This mixture works extremely well with roasted or barbecued pork.

Makes 1 x 2oz jar.

3 tablespoons coriander seeds
3 tablespoons cumin seeds
1 tablespoon black peppercorns
2 teaspoons red pepper flakes
2 tablespoons sea salt flakes
4 tablespoons granulated sugar
3 tablespoons dark brown sugar

1 small jar

In a dry frying pan, lightly toast the coriander and cumin seeds until just fragrant, about 30 seconds. Then, with a mortar and pestle, pound together the coriander, cumin, and peppercorns until you have a fairly coarse mixture. Stir in the red pepper flakes, salt, and sugars. Pour into a small jar and leave for a week for the flavors to blend.

Both of these rubs keep, sealed in a jar, for up to 3 months.

GROWING MYRTLE Myrtle, *Myrtus communis*, with its glossy, evergreen leaves and pretty white flowers, is an attractive addition to any garden. Plant it in well-drained, fertile soil in a sunny spot. It can be quite tender, so cover it in fleece during the worst of the winter frosts. Alternatively, plant it in a large pot and bring indoors for the winter. Be careful not to over-water myrtle—it hates soggy feet—and prune it lightly in spring to retain an attractive shape. All parts of the plant are fragrant. Used sparingly, the spicy, sweet leaves are an interesting alternative to bay leaves and the flowers can be tossed into salads. You can also substitute the shiny black berries for juniper. Don't discard your prunings, as the wood adds a delicious aroma to the grill. The leaves are also very good in potpourri (see page 89).

Herbal bathtime "teas"

These teas aren't a warming infusion which you sip while you bathe—though they do smell good enough to drink; rather they're fragrant little sachets to drop into your bathwater. Each blend makes about 8 sachets.

SLEEPY BLEND
10 tablespoons dried chamomile
5 tablespoons dried lavender

MOROCCAN SPICE BLEND
6 tablespoons dried rose petals and/or buds
3 tablespoons dried lemon verbena
2 tablespoons dried mint
1 thumb of fresh ginger, approx. 3in long, peeled and grated
6 cardamom pods, roughly crushed
Finely grated zest of 1 small orange
1/4 teaspoon ground cinnamon

Muslin
Small, tie-on gift tags (optional)
Needle and thread or sewing machine

Mix all the ingredients together in a bowl, or in two bowls if you are making both versions.

Cut out 16 (or 32) 4in squares of muslin. Write the name of the blend on the gift tags, if using. Place two squares of muslin together and, either by hand or with a sewing machine, sew around three sides of the squares about a quarter of an inch from the edge. Spoon a couple of tablespoons of the mixture into the resulting bag. Sew together the final side, making sure you catch the string from the gift tag in the stitching, if using. Make the rest of the bags in the same way.

An alternative way to make the sachets is to cut the muslin into circles about 6in in diameter, place the herbal blend in the middle, gather the edges together and tie up securely with string.

Stored in an airtight container, the "teas" will retain their fragrance for a couple of months.

GROWING CHAMOMILE

Chamomile, *Chamaemelum nobile*, is a deliciously sweet-scented perennial herb renowned for its calming properties. Both the leaves and flowers are strongly aromatic. It thrives in well-drained, light, fertile soil in a sunny spot, though it will tolerate some dappled shade. Sow the seeds in spring, scattering them on the ground and covering them with a thin layer of soil. Water well in dry spells and harvest the flowers in summer when they are fully open. After a couple of years, lift plants in the spring and divide them to promote vigorous growth (see page 10). *C. nobile* is also known as the "plant physician," as it is said to strengthen the growth of neighboring plants.

Herb cushion

Certain herbs have long been associated with promoting calm and peaceful sleep. A small pillow filled with hops, lavender, and chamomile, either singly or in combination, is a wonderful addition to any bedroom. Herb cushions make great gifts for frequent travelers too, as they are soothing on long flights and provide a welcome touch of home in strange hotel rooms. Makes 1 cushion, approx. 9 x 12in.

2 tablespoons dried hops
2 tablespoons dried lavender
2 tablespoons dried chamomile

2 pieces muslin, approximately 9 x 12in
About 36in covering fabric
Ribbons or bands of contrasting fabric for trimming
 (optional)
Needle and thread or sewing machine

Combine the hops, lavender, and chamomile in a bowl. You may wish to alter the balance of ingredients slightly until you get a combination which you particularly like.

Pin the muslin rectangles together and sew around three and a half sides, either by hand or using a machine, approximately half an inch in from the edge. Turn out the cushion liner and stuff with the filling. Sew up the opening.

To make the cover, cut out one piece of fabric measuring 10 x 13in to form the front of the pillow. If you want to sew on decorative bands of contrasting fabric or ribbon, it's easier to do that now. Cut out two pieces of fabric measuring 10 x 8in. On the two smaller pieces, turn over the shorter edge by half an inch, press and stitch to form a hem.

Place the larger piece on the table, right-side up. Place the shorter pieces on top, overlapping and with the right-sides down, with the hemmed edges toward the middle (when you turn the pillow out, these will form the opening). Pin then stitch, about half an inch in from the sides. Trim off the corners, turn out, and press. Stuff with the herbal cushion.

GROWING HOPS

Hop, *Humulus lupulus*, is a twining herbaceous perennial which will ramble and climb along wires or across a pergola, providing a striking screen of green. In late summer, female hops bear attractive, papery, lime-green cones which you can dry and use as garlands in the house or to fill pillows. To ensure vigorous growth, plant hops in well-drained, deep, rich soil in a sunny spot, though they will still do pretty well in clay and will tolerate some shade. Plant in winter when the plant is dormant and cut down in fall to encourage strong growth the following year. *H. lupulus* 'Aureus', the golden hop, is a particularly attractive variety, with deeply lobed yellow leaves.

Fabric conditioner

A bottle of fabric conditioner may seem like an odd gift, but combine it with a Moth-banishing pelargonium (page 113) or Moth-repellent sachets (right) and it makes a thoughtful present for a fashion-conscious friend. Makes 1 pint.

Large bunch of basil or mint
Strip of orange, lemon, or pink or yellow grapefruit peel, pared with a vegetable peeler and any traces of white pith removed
1 pint distilled white vinegar
Pretty bottle

Vinegar not only softens clothes as well as any expensive fabric conditioner, it also helps to remove soap residue which can dull the colors of your clothes. Also, unlike commercial conditioners, it removes stubborn odors rather than simply masking them. And, as an added bonus, if you live in a hard-water area, using vinegar conditioner regularly helps to stop the build-up of limescale in your washing machine.

Crush the basil or mint gently in your hands to help to release its scent, then put the whole stems into a bottle with the strip of citrus zest. Top up with the vinegar.

Pour about half a cup into the conditioner dispenser of the washing machine for each wash.

Moth-repellent sachets

These little sachets are so simple to put together, they're a great creative project for children to make as gifts for clothes-loving godparents or relatives. Makes 8–10.

2 tablespoons dried wormwood
2 tablespoons dried lavender flowers
1 tablespoon dried mint
1 tablespoon dried rosemary

OTHER THINGS YOU CAN ADD
Dried pelargonium leaves (see page 113 for varieties)
Dried tansy
Dried lemon verbena
Whole cloves
Broken cinnamon sticks

Muslin or light cotton fabric
Tailor's chalk or a soft pencil
Pinking shears (optional)
Ribbon

Combine all of your chosen ingredients in a bowl.

Draw circles of 6in in diameter onto the fabric using chalk or a soft pencil—use a saucer as a template if you like. Cut out with pinking shears to create an attractive, non-fraying edge, or cut a straight edge with ordinary scissors. Place a couple of spoonfuls of the herb mixture into the center of each circle and tie into a little bundle with the ribbon.

The sachets will retain their moth-banishing abilities for up to a year, after which time they will need to be replaced.

GROWING BASIL Sweet basil, *Ocimum basilicum*, is a tender annual that needs plenty of sunshine and shelter to thrive. Sow the seed in spring directly into pots and cover with a very fine layer of soil, water and place on a sunny window sill. Put the pots outside in late spring when all chance of frost has passed. Keep pinching out the tips to prevent flowering and promote bushy growth and water in the middle of the day. When the air cools in fall, bring the pots inside and keep them in a bright corner of the kitchen so you can continue to chop at them into the winter. Some varieties you may like to try are *O. b.* var. *purpurascens*, or opal basil, which has highly fragrant, purple leaves, and *O. b.* var. *minimum*, or Greek basil, which is a compact, attractive little plant with small leaves and excellent flavor.

Antiseptic vinegar

This is a simple version of Four Thieves Vinegar, a concoction that was said to have been used by looters during the plague in 17th-century France to protect them from infections. Use it to clean kitchen surfaces or to soothe scrapes or small scalds. Makes 3 pints.

A small handful of each of the following fresh herbs/flowers:
Mint
Lavender
Rosemary
Sage
Thyme
Wormwood

3 pints cider vinegar or distilled white vinegar
Large jar/bottle with a vinegar-proof lid
Spray bottle or other bottle with vinegar-proof lid
Muslin
Funnel

Roughly chop or tear the herbs, then place in a large jar or bottle and pour the vinegar over to cover. Seal and place in a cool, dark place for 2 months, shaking every now and then.

Line a sieve with muslin and strain the infusion into a large pitcher. Use a funnel to decant into a spray bottle.

If putting the antiseptic directly on the skin, mix it half-and-half with distilled water. You can make this diluted version ahead of time and keep it in a sterilized dropper bottle for when you need it.

The vinegar will keep for up to a year in a cool, dark place.

Fragrant firelighters

A basket of natural "firelighters" makes a wonderful hostess or housewarming gift. Make them in the fall when you're pruning back your herb beds and shrubs and you should be able to make enough bundles to last through the winter.

GROWING EUCALYPTUS

Eucalyputus is a genus of more than 400 fast-growing evergreen trees. If you want branches that remain at a low-enough level to cut for flower arrangements and firelighters, you will have to be ruthless about cutting back the previous year's growth to ground level each spring and growing it as a shrub rather than as a tree. It prefers rich soil and full sun, though it is fairly hardy in temperate climates. If it looks as though it has died during a cold winter, be patient as new stems may well emerge in late spring. One of the easiest varieties to grow is *Eucalyptus gunnii*, or cider gum.

CUTTINGS FROM
Bay
Bergamot
Eucalyptus
Lavender
Lemongrass
Lemon verbena
Mint
Rosemary
Sage
Thyme

OTHER THINGS YOU CAN ADD
Strips of orange, grapefruit, lemon, or lime peel
Cinnamon sticks

Raffia or cotton string

Tie the cuttings up in small, mixed bundles with the raffia or string. Leave in a cool, airy place to dry out completely before using them. You could use a drying screen (see box on page 90) or simply hang them upside down from a coat hanger until dried, which should take a week or so.

Nourishing herbal face wash

As well as being beautifully fragrant, orange blossom water is a simple and effective skin cleanser. Combined with soothing herbs, it makes a gently foaming face wash which is particularly suitable for dry or mature skins. Look out for pretty bottles, especially those made from dark or opaque glass, to make this face wash and the other beauty products in this book into even more special gifts. Makes approx. 1 pint.

1 teaspoon dried mint or chamomile or
    thyme or borage leaves
2 teaspoons honey
$\frac{1}{2}$ cup orange blossom water
$\frac{1}{3}$ cup glycerine
$\frac{1}{3}$ cup liquid pure Castile soap
1 tablespoon witch hazel

Muslin
Funnel
Pretty bottle/s

Place the dried herbs in a small pan with 1 cup of water. Bring to a boil, lower the heat, and simmer gently for a couple of minutes. Remove from the heat, stir in the honey, and leave to cool and infuse for an hour.

Line a sieve with muslin and strain the infusion, squeezing the muslin to extract as much of the herbal water as possible. Mix with the rest of the ingredients, then pour through a funnel into the cold, sterilized bottle/s.

The face wash will keep for up to 2 weeks.

GROWING HERBS AND FLOWERS FOR BEAUTY TREATMENTS OR COOKING

It's very important that leaves or petals you intend to use on your skin aren't sprayed with pesticides or other harmful chemicals. Research natural methods of pest control such as vigilant "housekeeping" companion planting and organic sprays.

Herbal vinegar hair rinse

Rinsing once a week with cider vinegar is an excellent way to remove product build-up on hair, leaving it soft and glossy. A hair rinse is a particularly good gift for a friend who lives in a hard-water area, where calcium in the water can make the hair flat and dull. Combined with a bottle of Herbal Face Wash, this makes a very good pampering present. Makes approx. 1 1/2 cups.

1³/₄ cups cider vinegar

ONE OF THE FOLLOWING
2 teaspoons fresh sage leaves (good for weak, dull, or dry hair)
2 teaspoons fresh rosemary leaves (good for dark or oily hair)
2 teaspoons fresh chamomile flowers and leaves (good for fair hair or irritated scalp)
2 teaspoons fresh marigold petals (good for dull or dry hair)

Muslin
Funnel
Bottles with vinegar-proof lids

Place the vinegar and your chosen herbs or flowers in a small pan and bring to just below boiling point. Leave to cool and infuse overnight. Line a sieve with muslin and strain the vinegar through it. Use a funnel to decant into cold, sterilized bottles and seal with vinegar-proof lids.

To use the hair rinse, massage about a cup of the rinse into freshly shampooed hair, leave for a minute and then rinse well.

The hair rinse will keep for up to 4 months.

SAGE AS A COMPANION PLANT

It's a good idea to plant sage alongside carrots and brassicas as it deters carrot fly and cabbage moth. Its flowers also attract bees and other beneficial insects to the garden.

GROWING LAVENDER IN CONTAINERS

Many types of lavender grow well in pots. Container growing is particularly suitable for more tender varieties such as *Lavandula canariensis*, *L. viridis*, *L. pedunculata*, or *L. pinnata*, which need to be brought inside during winter in colder climates. Good drainage is very important, so make sure there are broken crocks in the bottom of the pot and mix some extra coarse grit or pea gravel in with the potting soil. Feed with liquid fertilizer during the flowering season but water sparingly in the winter, allowing the soil to dry out almost completely between waterings.

Sugar body scrub

This body scrub is very simple to make but feels enormously luxurious to use, like something you might find in an exclusive spa rather than in your kitchen cabinets.

Makes 1 x 9oz jar.

$^3/_4$ cup superfine sugar
$^1/_4$ cup raw natural sugar
3 teaspoons dried rose petals
3 teaspoons dried lavender flowers
8–10 drops rose essential oil
8–10 drops lavender essential oil
$^1/_3$ cup sweet almond or jojoba oil
1 tablespoon glycerine

1 x 9oz jar

In a bowl, whisk together the sugars, rose petals, and dried lavender. Sprinkle on the essential oils and mix. Trickle over the almond or jojoba oil and glycerine and stir until well mixed. You may want to add slightly more almond oil until you get the texture you want. Scrape into a cold, sterilized jar with a spatula and seal.

The scrub can be used all over your body, but is particularly effective on hands, feet, and dry patches such as elbows and knees. Massage in for a minute or two, then rinse off.

The scrub will keep, sealed, for up to a year.

Lavender nail oil

Nourishing lavender oil rubbed regularly into the cuticles helps to keep nails healthy. This makes a thoughtful present for an avid gardener—we all know that, despite our best intentions, many of us forget to wear gloves during long hours toiling in the garden and our hands can suffer as a result. Makes approx. 1 cup oil.

1$\frac{1}{4}$ cups sweet almond oil
3 tablespoons dried lavender
4 vitamin E capsules

Muslin
Pretty bottles

Pour the almond oil into a pan with the lavender. Warm over very low heat until small bubbles appear at the edges of the pan. Keep the heat as low as you can, stirring from time to time, and continue to warm for 20 minutes—you don't want to boil the oil, you're simply infusing it with the lavender. Remove from the heat and leave to cool and infuse overnight.

Line a sieve with muslin and place it over a bowl. Strain the oil, pressing down on the lavender to extract as much of the oil as you can. Pierce the vitamin E capsules with a pin and stir the contents into the lavender oil. Pour into cold, sterilized bottles.

The oil will keep for up to 4 months.

REVIVING NEGLECTED LAVENDER PLANTS

Though lavender is fairly simple to grow, without a small amount of regular attention plants can become straggly. In late spring, when the plant begins to put on new growth, cut back the shooting stems by about a third, being careful not to cut into old wood as this won't revive. In early fall, trim lightly into shape again.

Lavender bath salts

The minerals in sea salt and Epsom salts help to soothe tired muscles and the lavender relaxes a weary mind. This makes a very good gift for anyone going through a trying time. Makes approx. 1¹/₃lbs.

10¹/₂oz sea salt
10¹/₂oz Epsom salts
2 tablespoons rosehip oil
8 drops lavender essential oil
2 tablespoons dried lavender flowers

Glass jars

In a large, wide bowl combine the sea salt with the Epsom salts. Sprinkle on the rosehip oil and lavender essential oil and mix with your hands until well combined. Scatter the dried lavender over the top and mix again. Spoon the salts into cold, sterilized jars and seal.

A handful or two of the salts scattered under running water is enough for a relaxing bath.

The salts will keep well for a year.

LAVENDER TROUBLESHOOTING

If your lavender isn't as full and healthy as you would like it to be, it's probably down to two things: soil and location. In the right conditions, it isn't a demanding plant to grow, so give yourself the best chance of success by picking the sunniest spot you can and, if your soil is at all heavy, prepare the ground by digging in some grit or sand to provide it with the fast-draining conditions it loves. Planting lavender near a wall gives it some added warmth and protection from harsh winds in winter.

LAVENDER AS A COMPANION PLANT

Lavender attracts bees and other beneficial pollinating insects to the garden and it is thought to confuse some moths and aphids with its strong scent. It is believed that planting lavender near fruit trees may help to deter codling moth.

PACKAGING IDEA Tie a wooden or aluminum scoop to the jar with a pretty ribbon.

Lavender ironing spray

Anything which makes this humblest of household tasks more enjoyable is surely to be welcomed. This also makes a very good, refreshing room spray. If you have handfuls of lavender in the garden, you can make a simple infusion. For a stronger-smelling spray, add some essential oil and a splash of vodka to help it disperse evenly throughout the liquid; this version also has a longer shelf life, which may be important if you are planning to give it as a gift. Moths hate the smell of lavender, so if you know someone who is suffering from an invasion of these greedy pests, give them a bottle of this spray teamed with some Moth-repellent Sachets (page 35) for a doubly effective present. Makes approx. 2½ cups.

4 tablespoons dried lavender flowers and leaves
10 drops lavender essential oil
2 tablespoons vodka

Coffee filter paper
Funnel
1 x 25oz bottle, for storing
Spray bottle, for using

Put the lavender into a pitcher and pour in 1 cup of lightly simmering water. Leave to steep for 5 minutes, then strain through the filter. Add an additional 1½ cups of boiling water.

Pour through a funnel into a cold, sterilized bottle. Add the essential oil and vodka and give everything a good shake. Decant into a spray bottle before using for ironing. The simple infusion will keep in the fridge for up to 10 days. The stronger spray will keep for up to a month.

Lavender hand warmer

A cozy wool hand warmer can make even the coldest day seem a little less daunting and is a great winter gift.
Makes 1 hand warmer.

8 x 16in medium-to heavy-weight
 wool fabric or tweed
Ceramic pie weights
4 tablespoons dried lavender
Embroidery thread

Needle and thread or sewing machine

Cut out the fabric into two circles or ovals, approximately 6in in diameter. Pin the fabric together and sew, about $1/2$in in from the edge, leaving a gap of about 2in in the stitching. Snip toward the stitching at intervals to help it lie flat when turned out.

Turn the handwarmer out to the right side and press. Fill fairly loosely with the pie weights—you don't want the hand warmer to be too full, as it needs to sit comfortably in the hands. Spoon in the lavender. Sew together the opening securely.

Use the embroidery thread to create an attractive blanket-stitch border around the edge of the hand warmer. If blanket stitch seems a little ambitious, a simple line of running stitch about $1/2$in in from the edge looks very good too.

To warm the hand warmer, place in the microwave at full power for $1^1/2$ minutes. Do not leave unattended while warming.

How To DRY LAVENDER

Harvest your lavender on a sunny day after the morning dew has evaporated. Cut the stems just above the leaves when the flower buds have good color and are just about to open—this is when they smell strongest. Tie them in bundles with elastic bands and hang them upside down in a dark, dry place to help preserve their color and scent. The buds should take a couple of weeks to dry.

LAYERING LAVENDER

Propagating lavender by layering is a good way of increasing your supply of plants. In early fall, select a long, vigorous stem and bend it toward the ground. Hold it in place with a hoop of wire pressed firmly into the earth and cover with about a quarter of an inch of soil. The following spring, when you see signs of new growth, cut the layered plant from its parent plant and pot it. Plant the following fall. (See page 11.)

Lavender wine jelly
This jelly is delicious served with roasted lamb or pork. Makes approximately 5 x 8oz jars.

3¹/₂lbs cooking apples
1¹/₄ cups white wine
3 tablespoons dried lavender, plus
   dried lavender sprigs for finishing
Granulated sugar
Juice of 2 lemons

Preserving pan or large,
   nonreactive pan
Jelly bag, plus extra muslin
Glass jars with lids or cellophane covers
Waxed disks

Roughly chop the apples—you don't need to peel or core them. Place them in a large saucepan with just enough water to cover. Bring to a boil, reduce the heat and then simmer, covered, until the apples are very soft; this should take 45 minutes to an hour. Suspend a jelly bag over a bowl and put the apples into it. Leave them to drip overnight.

Pour the wine into a pan with the lavender (not the sprigs), bring to a simmer, remove from the heat, and strain through muslin. Place a saucer in the freezer to chill.

Pour the lavender-infused wine into the strained juice from the apples and measure. For every 2 cups of juice, weigh out 1lb of sugar. Put the sugar and juice into a preserving or other large pan and warm over medium heat, stirring from time to time, until the sugar has dissolved. Bring to a rolling boil and boil until the setting point is reached, about 15 minutes. It's reached the setting point when you drop a teaspoonful onto the chilled saucer and it wrinkles when you push it with your finger.

Remove from the heat and skim to remove any scum. Stir in the lemon juice. Pour into warm, sterilized jars and add a lavender sprig to each jar. Cover the top of the jelly with waxed disks and then seal the jars with either cellophane covers or screw-on lids.

Stored in a cool, dark place, the jelly will keep for a year.

THE BEST CULINARY LAVENDER

Used sparingly, lavender adds a fragrant depth of flavor to sweet and savory dishes. Not all lavenders are equal, however, at least when it comes to cooking. If you're growing lavender for the kitchen, stick to English lavender, *Lavandula angustifolia*. Its sweet, slightly citrusy scent and lower camphor content make it the cook's lavender of choice.

STERILIZING JARS & BOTTLES When making any kind of preserve, it's essential that the jars or bottles are scrupulously clean. Either use jars and lids while they're still hot from the dishwasher or, if you don't have a dishwasher, boil them in plenty of water for a minimum of 10 minutes. Cleaned jars can be kept warm in a low oven until you're ready to use them. In some cases, such as when you're making drinks or pickles, you need to use cold jars or bottles—sterilize them first then allow them to cool. Chutneys, pickles, and any preserves with a high acidic content need to be sealed with vinegar-proof lids.

Herb-scented oils

Infusing light oils with herbs and spices is a wonderful way to add instant flavor to salad dressings, roasted vegetables, and pizzas. Or you can simply pour the oil into a dish with a little well-flavored vinegar and use as a dipping oil for bread. Makes approx. 2$\frac{1}{3}$ cups.

2$\frac{1}{3}$ cups light olive oil or sunflower oil
1 teaspoon mixed peppercorns (optional)

FOR ROSEMARY OIL
6–8 sprigs of dried rosemary

FOR THYME OIL
6–8 sprigs of dried thyme or lemon thyme

FOR CHILE OIL
1 teaspoon red pepper flakes
3 whole dried chiles

1 x 18oz bottle or 2 x 9oz bottle/s
Labels

Pour the oil into a heavy-bottomed saucepan and add the peppercorns, if using, and your chosen flavoring. Warm the oil gently over medium heat just until bubbles appear around the edge of the pan.

Remove from the heat and leave to cool. Pour the oil through a funnel into one or two sterilized bottles. Add the seasonings to the bottle too. Seal, label, and leave in a cool, dry place.

The oils will keep in a cool, dry place for 2 months.

SAFETY
Don't be tempted simply to add fresh herbs to oil unless you are planning to refrigerate the oil and use it within 5 days. Using fresh herbs in the oil can lead to the growth of harmful bacteria and is potentially very dangerous.

PACKAGING IDEA Tie some beautiful salad servers to a bottle of flavored oil, or give a bottle or two with a salad bowl for an extra-special gift.

GRoWING RoSEMARY

It is impossible to imagine an herb garden without rosemary. *Rosmarinus officinalis*, the woody, evergreen hardy perennial, is native to the Mediterranean, so it thrives best in light, well-drained soil where it can bask in sunshine. In spring, after it has flowered, trim it back enthusiastically to ensure bushy growth. In winter, in cooler, less well-sheltered places, it's a good idea to mulch the area around your rosemary to protect it from frost. There is a rosemary for every spot. *R. o.* 'Miss Jessopp's Upright' is a vigorous, bushy variety which makes a splendid hedge; *R. o.* Prostratus Group has a spreading habit, which makes it good for planting in walls, containers, or hanging baskets.

Rosemary moisturizing lotion
This lightly scented cream can be used on the body but is gentle enough to use on the face too. Makes approx. 8oz.

1 tablespoon fresh rosemary leaves
$1/2$ cup sweet almond or jojoba oil
1 tablespoon beeswax, grated
1 tablespoon honey
2 tablespoons rosehip oil
$1/4$ teaspoon benzoin tincture (a natural preservative)
2 x 4oz dark glass jars

Muslin

Place the rosemary leaves in a small pan with about half a cup of water. Bring to a boil, reduce the heat, and simmer for 5 minutes. Remove from the heat and leave to infuse for 4 hours.

Place a small heatproof bowl over a pan of barely simmering water; the bottom of the bowl should not touch the water. Pour the almond or jojoba oil into the bowl with the beeswax. Warm, stirring from time to time, until the wax has melted. Remove the bowl from the heat, whisk in the honey, and cool to room temperature. Stir in the rosehip oil.

Place a sieve over a pitcher and line with muslin. Strain the rosemary liquid into a pitcher and stir in the benzoin tincture. Spoon the oil mixture into a food processor or blender and process for a minute. With the motor still running, pour the rosemary infusion through the feed tube and process until you have a smooth emulsion. Transfer the cream into cold, sterilized jars and seal.

This cream will keep in the refrigerator for 2 weeks.

GROWING ROSEMARY FROM CUTTINGS
Rosemary is tricky to grow from seed, but you can increase your supply of this most valuable of herbs by propagating with cuttings. Take softwood cuttings of 4–6in long from the new wood in spring. Remove the leaves from the bottom of the stem, leaving only about six leaves at the top. Prepare a pot with well-draining potting soil to which you have added some pea gravel and proceed as for Taking Softwood Cuttings (page 9).

PROPERTIES OF ROSEMARY
Rosemary has strong antiseptic and anti-inflammatory properties. It improves blood flow and refreshes the mind. It is used in beauty preparations to condition the scalp and hair, tone and balance oily skin, and reduce puffiness. Its bracing scent uplifts and helps shake off sluggishness, which makes the moisturizer and toner very good for perking up the complexion in the morning.

Rosemary hair oil

This is an intensely nourishing and moisturizing hair treatment, perfect for dry, damaged hair. It makes a good gift for anyone who has returned from a summer beach vacation, when the combined effects of sun, salt, and chlorine can leave the hair in less-than-pristine condition.

Makes 1 cup of oil, enough for 5–6 applications.

1 cup coconut oil
4 tablespoons rosemary leaves stripped from the stalks
4 drops rosemary essential oil
7oz bottle

Muslin
Funnel

Place the oil in a small pan with the rosemary and bring to a bare simmer over low heat. Continue to poach the rosemary very gently for 5 minutes, then remove the pan from the heat. Leave to cool and infuse for 24 hours. Line a sieve with muslin and place over a bowl. Strain the infusion into the bowl and stir in the essential oil. Decant into a cold, sterilized bottle using a funnel.

To use the oil, warm a couple of tablespoonfuls either in the microwave (be careful not to get it too hot) or in a glass placed in a bowl of hot water. Wet the hair thoroughly with warm water and massage in the oil, starting at the scalp and working it through to the ends. Cover the hair with a shower cap and relax for 30 minutes before shampooing the treatment out and rinsing well.

The oil will keep in a cool, dark place for a month.

PACKAGING IDEA Pack a bottle of rosemary toner and a jar of rosemary moisturizer into a box or basket with a small rosemary plant. Tie a tag to the plant pot with suggestions for what to do with the sprigs. Aside from the usual culinary uses, a sprig or two tied in a bundle under a running hot tap infuses bathwater with its refreshing, enlivening scent.

Rosemary toner

This refreshing toner is a great way to wake up the skin in the morning and is particularly beneficial to oily skin.

Makes approx. 18oz.

1¼ cups rose water
1 small strip of orange zest, pared with a vegetable peeler, all traces of white pith removed
3 sprigs of mint
2 small sprigs of rosemary
1 cup witch hazel
¼ teaspoon benzoin tincture (a natural preservative)
2 x 9oz dark glass bottles

Muslin
Funnel

Place the rose water, orange zest, mint, and rosemary in a small pan. Warm over medium heat and let it cook at a bare simmer for 5 minutes. Remove from the heat and leave to infuse for 4 hours. Line a sieve with muslin and pour the infusion through it into a bowl. Whisk in the witch hazel and benzoin tincture. Use a funnel to decant into cold, sterilized bottles.

Use cotton-wool pads soaked with some of the toner to cleanse the skin.

The toner will keep in the refrigerator for 2 weeks.

Scented wax polish

Of course, you can use drops of essential oils to scent your wax polish, but if you have handfuls of herbs in the garden, you can use them to infuse the wax. Strongly scented herbs such as lavender, lemon verbena, and rosemary not only smell delicious, but they deter insects too. Makes 1 x 11oz jar.

1 cup jojoba or apricot kernel oil
3 teaspoons dried lavender, lemon verbena, or rosemary
2 strips of lemon zest, pared with a vegetable peeler,
   all white pith removed
3oz beeswax, grated
6 drops lavender or lemon essential oil
Can or glass jar
Muslin

Place the oil and dried lavender or herbs and zest in a small pan and warm over very low heat until tiny bubbles just appear around the edge of the pan—do not let it boil. Heat very gently for 5 minutes. Remove from the heat and leave to infuse overnight.

Strain the infused oil through a fine sieve lined with a single layer of muslin into a heatproof bowl which is the right size to fit over one of your pans. Fill the pan with a few inches of water—the water shouldn't touch the bottom of the bowl—and bring to a gentle simmer. Place the wax in the bowl with the infused oil and place the bowl over the pan. Warm gently, stirring from time to time, until the wax and oil have melted together and are well blended. Stir in the essential oil.

Pour the polish into a can or jar. If using a glass jar, warm it in a low oven for a few minutes immediately beforehand to stop it from cracking when the hot wax is poured in.

To use the polish, rub on a small amount—a little goes a very long way—and buff to a sheen with a soft cloth.

The polish keeps for up to a year.

GROWING LEMON VERBENA

Lemon verbena, *Aloysia triphylla*, is a highly useful and versatile herb, worth growing not only because it's very attractive, but also because it's almost impossible to buy commercially. Lemon verbena is a half-hardy deciduous perennial. It comes from Chile, so it likes warmth and should be protected from frost. Prune lightly after flowering and mulch around the base in winter to protect the roots from the cold. It will lose its leaves in winter, so don't be alarmed. Lemon verbena can be propagated from softwood cuttings (see page 9) taken in spring or from semi-hardwood cuttings taken in late summer (see page 54).

Tisane planter

Tisanes (herb infusions) are simple to make and a refreshing alternative to fermented teas. A planter crammed with infusible herbs makes a deliciously enticing gift.

GOOD HERBS FOR TISANES

Chamomile, leaves and flowers
Lavender, leaves and flowers
Lemon balm leaves
Lemon verbena leaves
Peppermint leaves
Rosemary, leaves and flowers
Sage, leaves and flowers
Thyme and lemon thyme, leaves and flowers

OTHER SUITABLE INGREDIENTS

Thin strips of lemon or orange zest,
    any white pith removed
Honey, for sweetening

Infusions of fresh herbs have a vitality that dried ones lack and you can choose your herb to match your mood. Peppermint is great after dinner as it aids digestion; lemon verbena, lavender, and chamomile are wonderfully soothing; rosemary is enlivening and sage is good for sore throats. You can use the herbs alone or in combination. Add strips of citrus zest if you like, and honey to sweeten.

To make a tisane, take a small handful of fresh leaves and blossoms and pour over about 2 cups of just-off-boiling water. Leave to infuse for 4–5 minutes before straining into a cup. Sweeten with honey if you wish.

GROWING LEMON VERBENA IN CONTAINERS

Lemon verbena, *Aloysia triphylla*, grows well in pots. Select a container that is at least 12in in diameter and keep the plant well watered during the growing season, feeding with liquid fertilizer once every couple of weeks. During the winter months, water only once every couple of weeks or so and discontinue feeding. Mulch around the plant in winter and move to a sheltered spot or cold greenhouse. In spring, prune back the previous year's growth to 2in.

A trio of tisanes

Making a special tisane (herbal tea) blend is a great way of showing a friend you're thinking of them.

Energizing
The perfect, uplifting tisane to combat that late-afternoon slump.

2 tablespoons dried peppermint leaves

1 teaspoon dried marigold petals

1 teaspoon dried ginger

2 pieces of dried lemongrass, roughly chopped

2 strips of dried orange zest, pared with a sharp vegetable peeler and all white pith removed

Dark-colored glass jars, pots, or airtight cans
Muslin and string (optional)

Calming
A soothing blend that helps promote sleep.

4 teaspoons dried chamomile

2 teaspoons dried lemon balm

1 teaspoon dried catmint

1 teaspoon dried lavender

1 teaspoon dried rose petals (optional)

Digestive
Serve this blend after dinner.

4 teaspoons dried peppermint leaves

2 teaspoons dried lemon verbena leaves

1/2 teaspoon fennel seeds

Make up your blend and pour into a dark-colored jar or an airtight tin to help preserve the flavor. Alternatively, cut some circles of muslin, spoon a couple of teaspoons of the blend into the center of each one and tie into bundles with string.

All tisanes are better made with water that has just been boiled, so let the water boil, then leave it for a couple of minutes before preparing the infusion, allowing a generous teaspoon of the blend per person and one for the pot.

The herbal teas will keep, stored in a cool, dark place, for a couple of months.

PACKAGING IDEA
Write out instructions for making the tisane on a gift tag. Add a pretty teapot and tea cup, with perhaps a jar of honey to sweeten the blend, to make this into a very special present indeed. If you were feeling very generous, add a tea strainer too.

GROWING LEMONGRASS
Zesty, invigorating lemongrass is essential to many Asian stir-fries and soups, but it's also very good in tisanes. It can be grown from seed, but it is a little finicky and you may need a heated propagator to ensure germination. Alternatively, and much more simply, take fresh, fat lemongrass stems you've bought from the supermarket and place them in a glass of water. As long as they haven't been over-trimmed, it's a fairly simple thing to get them to sprout roots. Once the roots are about 2in long, pot them and water thoroughly. Plants will thrive outdoors in full sun. Bring them inside in the winter, to either a sunny windowsill or heated greenhouse, and cut back on the watering—you want to keep the soil barely moist.

Lemon verbena jelly

This is a subtle and elegant jelly, suitable for a refined friend who may want something a little different for their toast. It's also delicious brushed on roast chicken toward the end of the cooking or added to pan juices to make gravy. Makes 4 x 8oz jars.

3 tablespoons lemon verbena leaves stripped from the stalks, plus 4 tablespoons of finely shredded leaves
2$\frac{1}{4}$lbs cooking apples, such as McIntosh or Pink Lady
Juice of 2 lemons
Zest of 1 lemon, pared in strips with a sharp vegetable peeler, all traces of white pith removed
Approx. 3 cups granulated sugar
Glass jars
Preserving pan or large saucepan
Jelly bag or muslin

Place 3 tablespoons of the verbena leaves in a pan with 1$\frac{1}{4}$ cups of water and bring to a boil. Boil for 1 minute then leave to cool and infuse. Strain through a sieve into a bowl. Discard the leaves.

Don't peel or core the apples; simply chop them into chunks and place them in a large saucepan with the lemon verbena infusion, lemon juice and zest, and just enough water to cover. Bring to a boil and simmer, partially covered, for an hour or so until the apples are very soft and pulpy.

Put the apples into a jelly bag and suspend over a bowl. If you don't have a jelly bag, place a large circle of muslin in a colander over a bowl, pour in the apples, tie up, and suspend over the bowl. Leave to drip for at least 4 hours or overnight. Place a couple of saucers in the freezer.

Finely chop the remaining whole lemon verbena leaves. Measure the juice and return to the clean preserving pan. For every 2$\frac{1}{2}$ cups of juice, add 1$\frac{3}{4}$ cups sugar. Heat gently, stirring, until the sugar has dissolved. Increase the heat and boil rapidly for 10–15 minutes until the setting point is reached. You can test this by dropping a teaspoon of the jelly onto a chilled saucer and pushing it with your finger— when it wrinkles, it's ready. Remove the pan from the heat, skim off any scum and leave to cool for 10 minutes. Stir in the lemon verbena leaves and put into warm, sterilized jars.

Mint jelly

There isn't a finer accompaniment to a leg of roasted lamb than this most traditional of English jellies. Including a pot of fresh mint makes this into an even more generous gift.
Makes approx. 5 x 8oz jars.

3$\frac{1}{3}$lbs cooking apples, such as McIntosh or Pink Lady
5–6 sprigs of mint, tied with kitchen string, plus approx. 3 tablespoons mint leaves removed from the stalks and finely shredded
1 cup cider vinegar or white wine vinegar
Approx. 3$\frac{3}{4}$ cups granulated sugar
Glass jars with vinegar-proof lids

Preserving pan or large, nonreactive saucepan
Jelly bag or muslin

Chop the apples into chunks—don't bother to peel or core them. Put them into a preserving pan or large saucepan with the bundle of mint sprigs and just enough water to cover. Bring to a boil and simmer, partially covered, until the apples are soft and pulpy, about 1–1$\frac{1}{2}$ hours. Add the vinegar and boil for an additional 5 minutes.

Put the apples into a jelly bag and suspend over a bowl. If you don't have a jelly bag, place a large circle of muslin in a colander over a bowl, pour the apples into it, tie up, and suspend over the bowl. Leave to drip for at least 4 hours or overnight.

Place a couple of saucers in the freezer. Measure the juice and return to the clean preserving pan. For every 2$\frac{1}{2}$ cups of juice, add 1$\frac{3}{4}$ cups sugar. Heat gently, stirring, until the sugar has dissolved. Increase the heat and boil rapidly for about 10–15 minutes until the setting point is reached. You can test this by dropping a teaspoon of the jelly onto a chilled saucer and pushing it with your finger—when it wrinkles, it's ready. Remove from the heat and skim off the scum with a slotted spoon. Stir in the shredded mint and cool for 10–15 minutes (this ensures the shredded mint will be distributed evenly through the jelly, and won't all rise to the top) before spooning into warm, sterilized jars. Put lids on immediately and store in a cool, dark place.

Both of these jellies will keep for up to a year.

Mint soap

If you're making a gift for a sleepy head, this combination of mint and ginger is guaranteed to wake up the senses during a morning shower. Makes approx. 4 soaps.

7oz glycerine melt-and-mold soap base,
   available online from soap-making suppliers
1 tablespoon dried mint
1 tablespoon peeled and grated fresh ginger
5 drops peppermint oil
Sweet almond or peanut oil, for greasing
   the molds

Water bath (optional)
Metal or silicone cake pans, or soap molds

Grate the soap base with the coarse side of a box grater and place in a heatproof bowl. Alternatively, use a water bath. Place the bowl over a pan of barely simmering water—the water should not touch the bottom of the bowl. Melt the soap, stirring from time to time, until it's liquid and well blended. Remove the bowl from the heat. Stir in the mint, ginger, and peppermint oil and mix thoroughly.

Lightly but thoroughly grease the molds with a little oil. Pour the liquid soap into a glass measuring cup and then into the molds. Rap the molds gently on the worktop to eliminate air bubbles (though this isn't necessary if you are using silicone molds) and leave to set for at least 4 hours.

If you're using silicone molds, simply press the soaps out. If using metal molds, use a small, sharp knife to help ease them out. Leave in a cool, dry place for 3–4 weeks to "cure" or harden before using.

gRowIng MINt

Members of the hardy perennial mint family (*Mentha*) flourish in moderately rich, moist soil in partial shade, though they will tolerate full sun so long as you can guarantee them enough moisture as they are thirsty plants. Mint can be invasive, so if space is an issue, plant your mint in a large pot or bucket with the bottom cut out and sink it into the ground to limit its creeping roots. In spring, divide established plants (page 10) and chop away at it ruthlessly during the summer to encourage new, fresh shoots. Mint will also hybridize promiscuously, so plant different kinds well away from one another.

PACKAGING IDEA Create a pampering mint-themed gift by packing up some of these soaps with a jar of Energizing Tisane (page 57) and some Moroccan Spice Blend Bathtime "Tea" (page 31).

DIFFERENT KINDS OF MINT

There are hundreds of different kinds of mint, though broadly speaking they divide into two groups: peppermint (*Mentha piperita*) and spearmint (*Mentha spicata*). Spearmint, or garden mint, is the one we use most often in the kitchen; it is the mint that we stir into sauces to go with roasted lamb or sprinkle over new potatoes or freshly cooked peas. Peppermint is more bracing and pungent. It is very good in teas and cocktails or summery soft drinks. Of the many other varieties, some you may wish to try are:

APPLE MINT (*M. suaveolens*) Has a distinct aroma of ripe apples. Good in fruity desserts.

CHOCOLATE MINT (*M. x piperata citrata* 'Chocolate') Attractive purple-green leaves and a clean peppermint flavor with a chocolaty accent. Delicious in chocolate desserts.

MOROCCAN MINT (*M. spicata* 'Moroccan') Has a slightly spicy aroma and is a very fine mint to infuse in tea or use in salads.

PINEAPPLE MINT (*M. suaveolens* 'Variegata') An attractive, variegated mint with a sweet, fruity flavor.

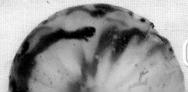

Catmint mice

These little mice will delight your feline friends.

Scraps of strong cotton fabric, corduroy or tweed
String or ribbon, for the tails
Hollow fill fiber toy stuffing, available from
   craft suppliers
2 teaspoons dried catmint for each mouse
Scraps of felt for the ears
Embroidery thread, for the eyes

Pins
Needle and thread or sewing machine

For each mouse, cut a heart-shaped paper template, approximately 7in at its widest point. Pin this to your fabric and cut around it. Cut the fabric heart in half along the central point so that you have two pieces. Place the right sides of the fabric together and tuck the tail in position so that you catch it as you sew around the mouse. Pin together and stitch, leaving a gap of about 1¼in in the base of the mouse. Turn the mouse right-side out and press.

Fill the mouse with the hollow fill fiber and a couple of teaspoons of dried catmint, then sew up the hole in the base securely. Cut small triangles of felt for the ears and stitch them on. Embroider small crosses for eyes. The catmint mouse's scent will remain strong for several months.

GROWING CATMINT

Hardy perennial catmint, *Nepeta*, gets its common name from the near-narcotic effect it has on cats, but it makes a very attractive border plant in its own right. Plant in well-drained soil in sun or light shade and when the first flowers have faded, cut right back to within a few inches of the soil line to encourage lush growth and a second crop of flowers. If you are cultivating it for your cat, you'll need to protect it. Cats will roll around on the plants in a state of ecstasy and gnaw the foliage down to the stems. Poking some twigs or sticks into the ground around the plant and tying some garden twine in a web between the sticks can help stop the worst of the damage.

Parsley dog biscuits

Giving people presents is one thing, but sometimes puppies need presents too. Parsley is famously good at sweetening the breath, which can only be a good thing.

Makes about 32 bones.

A big bunch of parsley, about 2 cups, finely chopped, stalks and all
1 large carrot, grated
1/2 cup Cheddar, or any other strong, hard cheese, grated
3 tablespoons olive oil
2 1/2 cups whole-wheat flour
approx. 3/4 cup hot chicken stock or water

3in cookie cutter, bone-shaped if possible

Preheat the oven to 350°F and line a couple of baking sheets with parchment paper.

Stir together the parsley, carrot, and cheese. Trickle over the oil and mix. Place the flour in a separate bowl. Add the parsley mixture into the flour and mix everything up with your hands until well combined.

Gradually add the stock or water, mixing until you have a good, stiff dough—you may not need to use all of the liquid. Knead it together gently with your hands, turn it onto a lightly floured surface and roll out until it's about 1/4in thick. Cut out the dog biscuits, using a cookie cutter. Knead any trimmings together, roll them, and cut them out too. Lay them on the baking sheets.

Bake for about 25 minutes until the biscuits are solid to the touch and turning golden around the edges. Cool on a wire rack.

Stored in an airtight container, the biscuits will keep for a couple of weeks.

GROWING PARSLEY

Hardy biennial parsley, *Petroselinum*, is possibly the most widely used of all the culinary herbs, so it's worth sowing in successive spring and summer plantings to guarantee a continuous supply. Plant in rich, well-drained soil in a lightly shaded spot. Keep cutting at your plants to ensure vigorous growth, trimming the larger, outer leaves first. *P. crispum* is the curly variety most often used as a garnish and *P. crispum neapolitanum* is an Italian flat-leafed variety with a stronger, more distinct flavor.

PACKAGING IDEA Why not use the cookie cutter as a useful and unusual gift tag?

GROWING CHAMOMILE FROM SEED

Chamomile Treneague (*Chamaemelum nobile* 'Treneague') and double-flowered chamomile (*C. nobile* 'Flore Pleno') can be propagated only by cuttings or division in spring, but Roman chamomile (*C. nobile*) is easily grown from seed. In early spring, sow the seeds finely in a prepared seed tray and cover with perlite. Provide warmth beneath the trays of 66°F with a heated propagating mat. Harden off and plant in late spring when all chance of frost has passed.

Chamomile bubble bath

This mixture can be poured under a running faucet to create a gently foaming, moisturizing bath. Castile soap is renowned for its mild, nonirritating, cleansing qualities. Traditionally made from olive oil, it's now also sometimes made with other plant-based oils. In its solid or liquid form, it's a very good thing to have in your gift-making kit as it can be used in many beauty and household preparations. Makes approx. 20oz.

4 tablespoons dried chamomile flowers
1 strip of orange zest, thinly pared with a vegetable
   peeler and all white pith removed
1 cinnamon stick
4$\frac{1}{2}$oz pure Castile soap, grated, or $\frac{1}{2}$ cup liquid
   Castile soap
3 tablespoons witch hazel
2 tablespoons glycerine
1 tablespoon powdered gelatine
Pretty bottles

Muslin
Funnel

Put the chamomile into a small pan with the zest, cinnamon stick, and 1$\frac{2}{3}$ cups water. Bring to a boil, lower the heat and simmer for 15 minutes. Strain through a sieve lined with muslin.

Add the grated or liquid soap to the infusion and stir until well combined, or until the grated soap has dissolved into the mixture. Stir in the witch hazel and glycerine. Sprinkle the gelatine over the top, leave for a minute, and then stir until completely dissolved into the mixture. When completely cold, pour through a funnel into cold, sterilized bottles.

The bubble bath will keep for 4 months.

Chamomile hair rinse

An infusion of chamomile will, with frequent use, help soothe an irritated scalp and bring out the natural highlights in blond hair, making it a suitable gift for fair-haired friends. Makes approx. 30oz, 3–4 applications.

4 teaspoons dried chamomile flowers
1 teaspoon marigold petals (optional)
$\frac{1}{2}$ teaspoon benzoin tincture (a natural preservative)
Pretty bottles

Muslin
Funnel

Place the chamomile and marigold petals, if using, in a pan with 1 quart of water. Bring to a boil and simmer, partially covered, for 15 minutes. Remove from the heat and leave the mixture to cool and infuse for 4 hours. Place a sieve over a bowl and line with muslin. Strain the infusion and whisk in the benzoin tincture, then decant into cold, sterilized bottles using a funnel.

After shampooing and conditioning the hair, pour a cupful of the rinse over the hair, starting at the roots and massaging it through to the tips. Leave the rinse in the hair and style as normal.

The hair rinse will keep in the fridge for up to a week.

Pretty can plant pots

Sometimes, either while away on vacation or shopping in well-stocked delicatessens, we buy tomatoes, puréed chestnuts, oatmeal, olive oil, and other foods in such pretty cans it seems a shame to toss them into the trash after using them. Give them a new lease on life as plant pots for herbs, small flowers, and cut-and-come-again salad leaves. They make an original gift for friends who only have a small amount of outdoor space, such as a balcony or windowsill.

A selection of tin cans
Pea gravel or broken crocks, for drainage
Potting soil
Herbs, cut-and-come again salad leaves, or
   small flowers such as pansies, pinks, and alpines

Hammer and large nail

If you can't find cans with pretty designs printed on the side, plain aluminum cans with the paper labels peeled off can also look surprisingly good.

Wash the cans and dry them. Turn them over and use the hammer and nail to punch a few drainage holes in the bottom. Put a thin layer of pea gravel or small crocks in the bottom for drainage, then add potting soil and pot your chosen plant.

Many plants will outgrow their cans eventually, but until they do they will make a striking display on a sunny kitchen windowsill, either indoors or out.

GROWING TARRAGON

French tarragon (*Artemesia dracunculus*) is, along with chervil, parsley, and chives, one of the *fines herbes* of classic French cooking. It's essential to béarnaise sauce, makes a very good seasoning for vinegar and is delicious with egg, fish, and chicken dishes. To grow it successfully in a small pot, give it a little shade, don't overwater it, and keep pinching off the leaves. When it outgrows its pot, plant it outside in light, well-drained soil in a sunny spot.

Edible wreaths

If you have abundant herbs and chiles in the garden at the end of the summer, preserve them in easy-to-make wreaths. Fresh, they make lovely green (or red) gifts which endure throughout the winter as the herbs and chiles dry and can be snipped off as required. The wire you need is available from good craft stores.

Generous handfuls of bay leaves, rosemary,
  sage, thyme
Red and/or green chiles

Heavy-gauge wire, available from florists, or an
  old wire coat hanger
Medium-gauge wire, available from florists
Disposable gloves, for handling the chiles
Pruning shears

Make a circle using the heavy-gauge wire, winding the ends together to bind. A diameter of about 8in works well—don't make it so large that you can't cover it generously with herbs and/or chiles.

Lay out the herbs on your work surface in separate piles. Divide each pile into fat little bunches. Cut lengths of the medium-gauge wire of approximately 6in. Tie each bunch of herbs together with the wire and then attach to the circle, overlapping them so that the stems and wire are covered, until you've completed the circle.

If you want to add chiles to your wreath, start by putting on your gloves, then thread pieces of wire through the top of each chile. Tie them into the wreath. Alternatively, chiles on their own make very striking wreaths. Simply thread medium-gauge wire through the tops of the chiles until you have a length of about 16in. Twine the ends together to fix into a circle.

GROWING SAGE

Common sage, *Salvia officinalis*, is native to the Mediterranean and thrives in well-drained soil in a spot where it will enjoy full sun for a good part of the day. Cut back the plant to about half its size after it has finished flowering to keep it vigorous. Though common sage is the version most often used in cooking, there are enormously attractive purple, variegated, and tricolor sages which look beautiful in the herb garden. They are milder in flavor than common sage and a little more tender, so may need protecting from harsh frosts in winter.

Sticky sweet cicely buns

Sweet cicely seeds add a hint of licorice flavor to these sticky buns. They're a delicious contribution to take along to a brunch or garden party. Makes 12.

1 tablespoon fresh sweet cicely seeds
3¹/₃ cups white bread flour
1 teaspoon salt
1 teaspoon ground cinnamon
¹/₂ teaspoon freshly grated nutmeg
1 package active dry yeast (about
   2 teaspoons)
Finely grated zest of 1 small orange
¹/₄ cup granulated sugar
¹/₃ cup butter, melted and cooled
2 free-range eggs, lightly beaten
²/₃ cup tepid milk

FOR THE FILLING
¹/₂ cup dried apricots
¹/₂ teaspoon ground cinnamon
¹/₃ cup brown sugar
¹/₂ cup pecans

FOR THE TOPPING
¹/₂ cup melted butter, plus extra for
   greasing the trays
¹/₃ cup honey, warmed, or
   maple syrup
¹/₄ cup brown sugar
³/₄ cup pecans, roughly chopped

2 baking sheets, 8 x 11 x 1in

Reserve 2 teaspoons of the sweet cicely seeds. Place the rest of the sweet cicely seeds on a cutting board and chop them finely with a knife. If they're more dried than green, pound them until fine using a mortar and pestle.

Sift the flour, salt, and spices into a large bowl. Whisk in the chopped sweet cicely, yeast, orange zest, and the sugar. Make a well in the middle, pour in the butter, eggs, and milk and mix until you have a soft dough. Turn onto a lightly floured surface and knead until silky and elastic. Place in a lightly oiled bowl, cover with a plastic bag and leave to rise until doubled in size. This takes 1–2 hours, depending on how warm your kitchen is.

To make the filling, put the apricots in a small bowl and add just enough boiling water to cover. Leave for 15 minutes, drain, pat dry, and roughly chop. Meanwhile, put the reserved whole cicely seeds into a food processor with the cinnamon, brown sugar and pecans and pulse until fine.

Turn the dough onto a lightly floured surface and knead it lightly for a minute. Divide it in two and roll each piece into an 8 x 12in rectangle.

Melt the butter for the topping. Brush some over the rectangles of dough and sprinkle half the nut mixture and half the apricots over each. Press the filling into the dough. Roll each rectangle up into a tight cylinder, starting at the widest end. Cut each roll into six pieces.

Brush the baking sheets with melted butter. Mix the melted butter, honey/syrup, and sugar together and spoon into the bottom of each sheet, spreading it out for an even coating. Scatter the nuts over. Put the buns in the sheets, leaving about 1in between each one. Cover with dish towels and leave in a warm place for 40 minutes until slightly risen.

Preheat the oven to 350°F. Remove the dish towels and bake the buns for 30–35 minutes until they are golden and feel firm. Immediately turn them over and place on a wire rack to cool.

The buns are best cooled, stored in an airtight container and eaten within a day of baking.

GROWING AND USING SWEET CICELY

It's surprising more of us don't grow this pretty, frondy, frothily-flowered herb. Sweet cicely, *Myrrhis odorata*, is a tall, hardy perennial which loves rich, well-drained soil and some dappled shade. Cut back the whole plant after flowering to encourage a fresh new growth of leaves.

All parts of the plant are edible. The long tap roots can be grated and eaten raw in a vinaigrette or rémoulade-type dressing, while the leaves have a sweet, licorice flavor and are good mixed into fruit salads or soft creamy cheeses and cucumber dishes. They're also a good addition to soups, stews, and omelets. Sweet cicely leaves make things taste sweeter, so they're very good with rhubarb, cherries, and other tart fruits because it means you can cut down on the sugar used to cook them. The green, unripe seeds taste a little like fennel seeds and impart a mildly spicy, fresh flavor to baking.

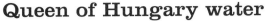

Queen of Hungary water

Legend has it that a magical concoction of herbs and flowers was created in the 14th century for Elizabeth, Queen of Hungary. More than just a perfume, it was drunk and massaged into skin as a cure for everything from rheumatism to gout. While I wouldn't recommend drinking this version, it makes a refreshing skin toner that helps to heal blemishes. In summer, keep a spray bottle of this scented water in the fridge and use it as a reviving spritz on hot days. Makes approx. 2 cups.

GROWING BERGAMOT

Bergamot, *Monarda*, is a clump-forming herbaceous perennial with dramatically pretty whorls of flowers that are highly attractive to bees, hence its common name, bee balm. Both leaves and flowers are highly fragrant. Young leaves and flowers are good in salads or potpourri, and a tisane of dried or fresh leaves soothes a sore throat. Start seeds off in trays and cover with a fine layer of perlite; providing some heat from beneath will help germination. When they're large enough to handle and all threat of frost has passed, transplant seedlings into pots and harden off before planting out about 20in apart. Alternatively, cultivate cuttings in summer (page 9, though there is no need to cover the cuttings with plastic) or root divisions in fall (page 10). Bergamot likes rich, moist, but well-drained soil in sun or partial shade. Cut down the stems in fall and divide the plant every 3 years or so to remove the dead center.

A handful of fresh rose petals
A small handful of fresh marigold petals
5 sprigs of rosemary
5 sprigs of bergamot
5 sprigs of peppermint
5 sprigs of lemon balm
5 sprigs of lemon verbena
2 sprigs of sage
A strip of orange zest, pared with a sharp vegetable peeler, all white pith removed
A strip of lemon zest, pared with a sharp vegetable peeler, all white pith removed
Approx. $1^2/_3$ cups vodka
Approx. $^1/_2$ cup rose water
Approx. $^1/_2$ cup witch hazel
Pretty bottles

Large glass jar

Layer all of the petals, herbs, and zests in a tall, sterilized jar. Pour over enough vodka to cover and leave on a sunny windowsill for a couple of weeks, shaking from time to time. Strain and measure the liquid. To each cup of liquid, add $^1/_2$ cup of rose water and $^1/_2$ cup of witch hazel. Decant into the cold, sterilized bottles.

The Queen of Hungary water lasts for up to 4 months.

PACKAGING IDEA Pack a generous bottle of Queen of Hungary water into a pretty basket with a perfume spray bottle, so the recipient can decant some of the mixture into it and keep it in the fridge as a sweetly scented enlivener.

Poppy anti-wrinkle wash

For centuries, poppy petals have been prized for their skin-soothing and smoothing properties. Combined with aloe vera, they produce a very good and gentle face wash for more mature skin. Makes approx. 1 cup.

A handful of fresh field poppy petals
³/₄ cup of orange flower water
4 tablespoons pure liquid Castile soap
2 tablespoons aloe vera gel
1 tablespoon glycerine
6 drops grapefruit seed extract (a natural preservative)
4 drops neroli essential oil
Dark glass bottle/s
Muslin

Place the poppy petals in a bowl and pour in enough boiling water to cover. Cover the bowl and leave for 4 hours.

Place a sieve over a pitcher and line with muslin. Strain the poppy liquid, then gently whisk in the rest of the ingredients. Pour through a funnel into cold, sterilized bottles.

The face wash will keep for up to a week out of the fridge, 2 weeks if refrigerated.

PACKAGING IDEA

Include a small pot of poppy seeds with the face wash. A teaspoon of seeds can be combined with a tablespoon or two of face wash to transform it into a gently exfoliating face scrub.

GRowING PoPPIEs

Field poppies, *Papaver rhoeas*, love sunshine and well-drained soil. They hate being transplanted. Sow them in spring and fall directly into the ground, cover them with a fine layer of soil, firm them in very gently and water well. When the seedlings are large enough to handle, thin them out to about 6in apart. Keep them well watered and dead head to prevent self seeding. Dry the seeds and use them in baking.

Thyme & fennel seed cleanser

Fennel seeds are very effective at reducing puffiness while thyme has a naturally astringent quality. This mild cleanser would suit any skin type. Decant it into a pretty bottle, which makes an enduring gift after the cleanser has been used up. Makes approx. 1 cup.

1 tablespoon fennel seeds
^{1}/$_3$oz fresh thyme sprigs
1 teaspoon honey
Juice of ^{1}/$_2$ lemon, strained
^{1}/$_4$ teaspoon benzoin tincture
   (a natural preservative)
8oz dark glass bottle

Mortar and pestle or spice grinder
Muslin or basket-type coffee filter
Small funnel

In the mortar and pestle or spice grinder, pound or blitz the fennel seeds until fine. Place in a heatproof bowl with the thyme sprigs and pour in 1 cup of boiling water. Cover and leave to infuse for 30 minutes.

Place a sieve over a measuring cup or bowl and line with muslin or a coffee filter. Strain the infusion, pressing down with the back of a spoon to extract as much of the liquid as possible. Whisk in the honey, lemon juice, and benzoin tincture and pour through a funnel into a cold, sterilized bottle. Seal and refrigerate.

The cleanser should be applied to the skin on a cotton pad and left for a minute or two before rinsing off with tepid water and patting dry with a soft towel.

This will keep in the refrigerator for a week.

GROWING THYME

There are hundreds of different varieties of thyme. All love well-drained, poor soil and plenty of sun, ideally in a spot where they'll be protected from harsh winter winds. Some of the smaller, creeping thymes, such as *Thymus serpyllum* 'Annie Hall', *T. s.* 'Lemon Curd' and *T. s.* 'Pink Chintz', are very good planted in gravel or in the cracks in concrete where they will spread in low mounds and scent the air as you brush past them. Common thyme, *T. vulgaris*, or lemon thyme, *T. citriodorus*, are the most useful in the kitchen. *T. citriodorus* has a sprightly lemon scent and both flowers and leaves are great in cooking, used as a refreshing tisane or added to potpourri (page 89). *T. c.* 'Golden King' is an excellent variegated variety. *T.* 'Doone Valley' is lemon-scented and, though it doesn't have such a fine flavor, in spring it is covered in very pretty flowers which, like all thyme flowers, are loved by bees. Propagate by cuttings or division in spring or summer (page 10), or by layering in fall (page 11). After flowering, give the plants a trim to encourage bushy growth and prevent them from becoming woody.

Simple table decorations

While it may be traditional to take a bunch of flowers as a gift for your host, your kindness may leave them with the headache of finding an appropriate vase just when they want to concentrate on pouring drinks and introducing guests. Small plants cultivated in your garden and planted in pretty pots make a very personal gift. As table decorations for your own dinner party, they benefit from being low in height so they don't distract, and you can even add labels to make them into fragrant place markers which guests can take home with them. Small flowers look good, though if they're going on the dining table it's best to avoid very strongly scented ones. Herbs make very pretty, inexpensive table decorations. You could even reflect the herbs used to season the meal. Use either low-growing herbs, such as thyme or chamomile, or tiny specimens of larger ones, such as bay or lavender.

PACKAGING IDEA

Old, weathered terra-cotta pots always look pretty, but use your imagination and you can use many easy-to-find containers for planting your table decorations. Jam jars, pretty cans, old bowls, or enamel mugs all look good. Simply fill the bottom with potting soil, pot your chosen plants and water lightly.

TAKING THYME CUTTINGS

There are over 300 varieties of thyme, and all are neat of habit, fragrant, and, when smothered in their tiny flowers, much beloved of bees—indeed, collecting different varieties of thyme can become something of an obsession. They are also easy to propagate from cuttings. In spring or early summer, take a softwood cutting (page 9) of about 3in and pot in potting soil. Bring the cuttings into the house or keep them in a cool greenhouse over winter and plant the following spring. Alternatively, creeping thymes are easy to divide. They put out aerial roots and form new little "plantlets" which can be dug up and planted in pots.

SUITABLE FLOWERS
Daisies (*Bellis perennis*)
Dwarf cyclamen
Dwarf irises
Grape hyacinths
Primroses
Snowdrops
Violets

SUITABLE HERBS
Basil
Bay
Chamomile
Chervil
Lavender
Lemon verbena
Thyme
Rosemary

Selection of planters
Potting soil

Pot your chosen plants and water lightly—if they are in containers with no drainage holes, you don't want to drown them.

The plants will be happy like this for a week or so. After that, they will need to be potted into containers that have drainage holes, or planted out in the garden.

Caraway flatbreads

These flatbreads taste very good with cheese or served with dips. They're a great gift to take along to an informal cocktail party. Makes about 24.

1³/₄ cups white bread flour, plus more for dusting
¹/₂ teaspoon baking powder
2 teaspoons caraway seeds
¹/₂ teaspoon sea salt flakes
A few grinds of black pepper
about 4 tablespoons of olive oil, plus extra for
  oiling the baking sheets

Preheat the oven to 325°F and lightly oil two baking sheets.

Sift the flour and baking powder together, then stir in the caraway seeds, salt, and pepper. Trickle the oil over the surface of the flour and rub it in with your fingers. Slowly pour in up to half a cup of cold water, mixing as you go—add just enough to make a soft dough. Knead lightly to ensure everything is well combined.

Lightly dust the work surface with flour and roll out the dough until it's about ¹/₄in thick. Use a wine glass or 2in pastry cutter dipped in flour to cut out circles of dough, then roll out each circle into a long, thin oval.

Place the ovals on the baking sheets and bake for about 5 minutes, until dry and crisp but still fairly pale. Cool completely on a wire rack and then store in an airtight container.

The flatbreads keep well for about 5 days.

gRowIng CARAwAY

Caraway, *Carum carvi*, is a hardy biennial which thrives best in rich, well-drained soil in full sun. The seeds are ready for harvesting in the plant's second summer. To harvest the seeds, cut the ripening seed heads off in the morning when the dew is still on them—this will stop the seeds from scattering as you gather them. Cover the seed heads with a paper bag secured with an elastic band and hang them upside down by their stems in a dry, well-ventilated place. The seeds will take about a week to fully dry out.

Drying flowers

Many flowers can be dried quite successfully by hanging them upside down in a warm, dark, and well-ventilated place, but using silica gel to dry them will preserve their colors and textures even better. Once dried, they can be used very effectively in wreathes, or wired into bouquets and table decorations.

SOME GOOD FLOWERS TO TRY

Anemones, asters, cornflowers, daisies, dahlias, delphiniums, freesias, grape hyacinths, marigolds, pansies, peonies, pinks, primroses, ranunculus, roses, snapdragons, zinnias

Silica gel, available from some craft stores and garden centers or online
Large plastic containers with airtight lids
Small, soft paintbrush

Pick the flowers on a dry day after the morning dew has evaporated. Select flowers when they're in as perfect condition as possible for the best results.

Pour a 1¼in layer of the gel into the bottom of a plastic container—use separate containers for each type of flower because they may dry at different rates. Place the flowers in the container and gently start to cover them, scattering the gel on gradually and shaking the container to ensure it covers every petal. Once the flowers are completely covered, put the lid on the container, making sure the seal is airtight.

It takes 2–5 days for most flowers to dry. Start to check after a couple of days and, once the flowers are dry, carefully take them out of the gel and remove any remaining granules with a soft brush.

Silica gel can be reused indefinitely. Follow the instructions on the package for reactivating it.

GROWING ANEMONES

The De Caen group of *Anemone coronaria* comes in a wide range of bright colors, from white to deepest purple, scarlet, and shocking pink. Their colors remain fairly true when dried in silica.

Plant in winter through to spring to ensure a succession of flowers. Soak the tubers in warm water overnight before planting in light, sandy soil to a depth of twice the height of the tuber and 4in apart. Mulch in the fall to protect the plants from frost.

GROWING PRIMROSES

Hardy herbaceous perennial primroses, *Primula vulgaris*, brighten up the early spring landscape with their pretty, lightly scented flowers. They will bloom cheerfully in many conditions but do best in well-drained soil in dappled shade. Trim off any dead leaves or blooms to prolong flowering and water well during spring and summer, less frequently from fall onward. Primroses grow very happily in pots and window boxes too.

Crystallized flowers

These make pretty and unusual gifts for avid bakers. Make sure you use flowers that have not been sprayed with pesticides or any other chemicals.

SOME LEAVES & FLOWERS SUITABLE FOR CRYSTALLIZING

Borage flowers
Dianthus flowers
Lavender flowers
Mint leaves
Primroses
Rose petals
Scented pelargonium leaves and flowers
Violas
Violets

1 egg white
Superfine sugar

Tweezers
Pastry brush or small, soft paintbrush
Sugar sifter or tea strainer

In a small bowl, lightly whisk the egg white together with 1 teaspoon of cold water. Hold the flower, petal or leaf you want to coat with tweezers and paint completely with the egg white, making sure the whole surface is covered.

Hold the flower, petal, or leaf over a baking sheet or some parchment paper to stop the sugar from going all over the work surface, then sprinkle the flower with sugar, using either a sugar sifter or tea strainer to scatter it evenly; make sure that the whole surface is covered. Shake off any excess. Place on baking sheets lined with parchment paper and leave in a warm, dry place for several hours or overnight to dry out completely.

Store in an airtight container, placing parchment paper between the layers of flowers, petals, or leaves to protect them. They will keep well for several months this way.

Decorated candles

Purchased candles decorated with dried flowers and leaves make wonderful gifts that you can tailor to their recipients. Herbs and leaves look very good in minimalist rooms, while a host of petals and flowers suit a more feminine or vintage interior. Delicate, fine foliage works better than fleshier examples.

Paraffin candle wax

Essential oils (optional)

Plain pillar or dinner candles (pale colors generally work best)

Delicate dried flowers and leaves (see Decorated Stationery, page 17)

Double boiler pan (the top part of the boiler should be deep enough for you to dip in the full length of the candle)

Candy thermometer

Tongs

Small paintbrush

Very soft, lint-free cloth

Paraffin wax is highly flammable, so choose a day when you can give the project your full attention. Select the dried flowers and leaves you want to use to decorate the candles and lay everything out before you start.

Put the wax in the top of your double boiler and put some water in the bottom. Place the candy thermometer in the pan. Heat gently, stirring with a long metal spoon occasionally, until the wax is completely melted. Paraffin wax has a melting point of 132–136°F. You can add a few drops of essential oils to scent your candles at this point if you like. Don't leave the melting wax unattended at any point, and when it's melted, remove from the heat.

When the wax has melted, dip the paintbrush into the wax and paint it around the parts of the candle you want to decorate. Gently press the flowers or leaves onto the candle, then brush a little wax over the top to fix it in place. Alternatively, carefully dip the leaves or flowers into the wax and place them on the candle, smoothing gently to adhere it to the candle.

Hold the candle by the wick (you may want to use tongs to do this) and quickly dip the entire candle into the wax to set the decorations. Cool completely and then buff gently to a sheen with a soft cloth.

Note: Never leave burning candles unattended.

Bouquets and boutonnieres

Natural bouquets of garden flowers are so much more enchanting than the small and contrived bunches available in many of the less imaginative stores. Spoiling your friends with the best your garden has to offer is really one of the most generous gifts of all.

CUTTING FLOWERS

The best time to cut flowers and branches is in the morning, while the dew is still on them. Cut them just before they are in full bloom and they will last longer in the vase. Immediately put them in a bucket of water in a cool, shady place for a few hours before arranging them.

To condition most flowers for arranging, use sharp garden shears to cut the stems again, about 2in from the base and on the diagonal so they will take up as much water as possible. Remove any leaves that will sit below the water line in the vase to limit the growth of bacteria which will shorten the life of your arrangement.

MAKING A SIMPLE BOUQUET

Strip the foliage from the lower parts of the stems. Hold three or four stems in your hand, arranging them at an angle so they begin to form a spiral. Layer in more stems, again at an angle, turning the bunch frequently to ensure it's a good shape. Hold in place with a rubber band, then tie tightly with raffia or ribbon. Trim the stems so that they're slightly longer in the center than at the edges.

BOUTONNIERES

Don't save boutonnieres just for weddings. And don't truss them up with the ungainly wire and tape used to torture commercial boutonnieres into obedience either. Choose flowers and foliage which won't wilt easily, and if you have to fix them with florist's tape, conceal it beneath thin silk or satin ribbon wound around the stems. Keep it simple. A few hydrangea blossoms, a cornflower, a single stem of lily of the valley will all look fresh and pretty. Or use herbs such as rosemary, a tiny fern frond, or some oak leaves and acorns.

GROWING PINKS

Pinks, *Dianthus*, are among the most beloved of the old-fashioned cottage garden plants, largely because of their deliciously sweet and slightly clove-like scent, which makes them a particularly good addition to potpourri. Plant in a sunny, well-drained spot and water in dry spells. Pinks become woody and sprawling after a while, so renew from cuttings in late spring. Gently tug away nonflowering shoots and trim just below a leaf joint. Put the cuttings around the edge of a pot filled with a mixture of one part potting soil to one part pea gravel and place in a shady part of the garden, uncovered. Don't overwater or the cuttings will rot. Once they are established, pinch out the tips to create bushy plants that can be planted in the soil in early fall.

Potpourri

Potpourri has had a bit of a bad rap in the past few years. Many commercial versions, smothered with artificial fragrances and dyed lurid colors, have all of the appeal of a plug-in air freshener. Making your own from the herbs and flowers in your garden is a different matter altogether. Delicately scented and subtly beautiful, it makes a wonderful present. For wet potpourri, look out for old-fashioned potpourri dishes with pierced covers to allow the scent to escape. For dry potpourri, any attractive dish will do. *For advice on highly-scented roses, see page 90.*

Wet potpourri

Wet potpourri mixtures take longer to make, though they are more intensely scented. When the perfume starts to fade, reactivate it by sprinkling on a few drops of brandy and stirring.

Handfuls of rose petals, gathered as the flowers
　come into full bloom
Coarse sea salt
2 tablespoons each of ground cinnamon, ground allspice,
　and ground nutmeg
1 tablespoon ground cloves
$2/3$ cup powdered orris root, a fixative available online
　or from natural food stores
Juice and the finely pared zest of 3 lemons
$1/4$ cup brandy
20 drops each of bergamot, lavender, and
　Rose Maroc essential oils
Large glass jar

During the course of the summer, layer rose petals and salt in a large glass jar—a handful of rose petals to a handful of salt. After a couple of months, mix together the spices, orris root, lemon juice and zest, and essential oils with the salted rose petals and any of the other dried flowers and herbs from the list (right). Sprinkle on the brandy. If the mixture seems too wet, sprinkle on some more orris root and mix. Return to the glass jar and store in a cool, dark place for a couple of months to mature before using.

Dry potpourri

This is the simpler mixture to make, though its scent fades more quickly than that of wet potpourri. It can be revived by sprinkling on more essential oils as needed.

3 tablespoons powdered orris root, a fixative available
　online or from natural food stores
1 heaping tablespoon benzoin gum powder, a fixative
　available online or from natural food stores
1 teaspoon ground cinnamon
30 drops each of bergamot, lavender, and
　Rose Maroc essential oils
$1/2$lb dried rose petals
$1/3$lb dried lavender flowers
Any dried flowers, herbs, and leaves from the list below
Large glass jar

Place the orris root, bezoin gum, and cinnamon in a small bowl and sprinkle over the essential oils. Rub them together with your fingers until well blended.

Combine the rose petals and lavender flowers in a bowl with any dried flowers, herbs, and leaves from the list below, then scatter over the essential oil mixture and stir until well combined. Store in a large glass jar in a cool, dark place for at least a month before using.

> **OTHER DRIED FLOWERS & HERBS TO INCLUDE**
> (for either the wet or dry potpourri): bergamot flowers and leaves, strips of citrus zest, honeysuckle, jasmine, lemon balm, lemon verbena, lavender flowers, myrtle, pinks, scented geranium leaves, sweet Williams, violets, and wormwood.

PLANTING
AND
DRYING
ROSES FOR SCENT

When growing roses for use in infusions, potpourri, or in cooking, it's important to choose strongly scented varieties. Seek out old roses such as albas, damasks, and gallicas, particularly *Rosa gallica* var. *officinalis*, also known as the apothecary's rose because of its ancient association with healing.

To dry the petals, pick the roses in the morning after the dew has evaporated. Gently pull the petals away from the base and lay them either on a drying screen (make one of these by stretching and stapling fine mesh to an old picture frame) or on a cooling rack. Leave them to dry for several days, turning them over from time to time. When they are completely dry and crisp, store the petals in an airtight glass container in a dark place.

Lip balm

These little pots of lip balm serve a dual purpose, as they work very well as a nail and cuticle cream, too. They're good gifts for well-groomed friends, particularly if you package them in shatter-proof containers—they're perfect to carry around in a handbag or briefcase. Makes approx. 8 pots.

½ cup sweet almond oil
2 tablespoons dried rose petals, dried mint, or dried lavender
5 tablespoons beeswax, grated
1 teaspoon honey
2 vitamin E capsules

Small glass, metal, or plastic pots or jars (1oz is a good size). If they're going to be left on a dressing table or in a bathroom cabinet, the sort of miniature jam jars that grace many a hotel breakfast are the perfect size

Place the oil in a small pan with the dried rose petals, mint, or lavender. Warm very gently over low heat for 5 minutes—do not let it boil. Cover and leave to cool and infuse for several hours or overnight. Strain into a small, heatproof bowl and discard the solids.

Place the bowl with the oil in it over a pan of barely simmering water—the water should not touch the bottom of the bowl. Stir in the beeswax and honey until everything is completely melted and blended. Remove from the heat, pierce the vitamin E capsules with a pin and squeeze the contents into the lip balm mixture. Pour into the pots, cool, and seal.

The lip balm will keep for 2 months.

Rose & oatmeal facial scrub

This is a very nourishing and beautifully scented facial scrub. Oatmeal removes impurities from the skin and is so gentle that it can be used on the most sensitive of complexions. Makes approx. 2oz.

1/4 cup rolled oats
2 tablespoons dried rose petals
4 drops essential Rose Maroc oil
Pretty jar

Place the oats and rose petals in a food processor or blender and pulse several times until the mixture is quite fine. Sprinkle on the essential oil and pulse once more to blend. Spoon into a cold, sterilized jar.

To use the scrub, combine a couple of tablespoons of the mixture with enough water to make a smooth paste. For very dry or sensitive skin, use milk in place of the water. Smooth onto the face and neck, leave for a minute, and then massage the scrub into the skin in gentle, circular motions. Rinse off with tepid water and pat dry with a soft towel.

The facial scrub will keep for 4 months.

DETERRING PESTS FROM ROSES

Planting any member of the onion family close to roses deters aphids as they become confused by their strong scent. They may lessen the chance of the leaves developing black spot too. Clumps of chives (page 23), allowed to flower, certainly look pretty among the roses and some believe that neighboring alliums intensify the perfume of roses too.

PACKAGING IDEA Write a label explaining how to use the facial scrub and tie it around the jar. If your intended recipient really loves roses, combine it with the Rose Milk Bath (page 94).

Rose water

Distilling your own rose water using things you probably already have in your kitchen is enormously satisfying and easy. The rose water on its own makes an original and generous gift, or whisk in a few more ingredients to create a gentle and nourishing cleanser. Makes approx. 29oz.

FOR THE ROSE WATER
Enough heavily scented rose petals to fill a 1-liter pitcher about three times (see page 90 for good scented varieties)

FOR THE CLEANSER
10oz rose water
1 tablespoon glycerine
1 tablespoon witch hazel
6 drops Rose Maroc essential oil

House brick
Large pan with a slightly domed lid
Heatproof bowl of at least 1-liter capacity
Bag of ice cubes
Funnel
Dark glass bottles

Place the brick in the middle of the pan and put the bowl on top of it. Scatter the petals all around the brick. Pour in just enough water to cover the petals and brick.

Cover the pan with the upside-down lid—inverting it lets the steam drip down into the bowl. Bring the water to a boil and immediately place a few handfuls of ice cubes on top of the pan lid. Lower the temperature and simmer the rose petals and water. The steam will rise, hit the inverted dome of the iced lid, condense, and drip down into the bowl.

Every 15 minutes or so, lift the lid and remove a teaspoon of the rose water in the bowl. It should smell and taste very strongly of roses. Don't let the petals simmer too long as their strength will start to decline after 40 or 50 minutes.

Carefully remove the bowl from the pan and place in a bowl of iced water to chill it as quickly as possible. Use a funnel to decant it into cold, sterilized, dark glass bottles and refrigerate.

To make the rose water cleanser, gently whisk together all of the ingredients and use a funnel to decant into cold, sterilized, dark glass bottles.

Both the rose water and rose water cleanser will keep in the fridge for up to a month.

ALTERNATIVE: JASMINE WATER
If you have an abundance of jasmine blossoms, you can use them in the same way to make a deliciously scented jasmine water. Decant this into a spray bottle and spritz it lightly on your face when you need a pick-me-up, lightly spray it on pillows before sleep, or use it as an uplifting room spray. See page 109 for advice on growing jasmine.

THE PROPERTIES OF ROSES
Many of us are familiar with the uplifting feeling of walking through a rose garden on a summer's day, breathing in the sweet and heady scent of the flowers. Rose essential oil has been used in beauty treatments for centuries, since not only does its aroma enhance well-being, but, applied to the skin in creams, lotions, and oils, it also reduces redness and is very beneficial to dry or sensitive complexions. While rose essential oils are expensive because of the enormous number of flowers it takes to make them, rose water (see left) is a mild and thrifty way of benefiting from the near-magical properties of roses. Though obviously not as intense as essential oil, it has excellent antiseptic, calming, and moisturizing qualities.

The prospect of pruning can make even experienced gardeners quite nervous. Take heart. When it comes to roses, a study by the Royal National Rose Society showed that taking a hedge trimmer to rose bushes and cutting off half of the top growth resulted in just as many blooms as conventional pruning. You probably don't want to take such drastic action with your precious shrubs, so there are a few simple rules to bear in mind.

Prune in early spring, just as the buds begin to swell, using sharp, clean garden shears. Start by removing any dead, weak, or damaged growth, ensuring you cut just above an outward-facing bud, sloping your cut away from the bud. Next cut out any weak or crossing stems. In many cases, it is enough to cut back the rose to about half or two thirds of its size. Old-fashioned non-repeating shrub roses need pruning only lightly to establish a good shape. For climbing roses, cut back the previous year's flowering shoots to about 8in and tie in the strong stems. Ramblers can be left to romp away at will, but you can thin out old growth as necessary and tie in new stems.

Rose Milk Bath

It's rather satisfying to think that two such humble ingredients as powdered milk and Epsom salts can contribute to such a luxurious, spa-worthy present. Dried milk moisturizes the skin while Epsom salts relax tired joints and, it is believed, draw out toxins from the body. Makes 12oz.

2 cups powdered milk
1/2 cup Epsom salts
12 drops essential Rose Maroc oil
2 tablespoons dried rose petals
Pretty, airtight bottles/jars

In a bowl, mix together the powdered milk and the Epsom salts. Sprinkle over the rose oil and mix to combine. Scatter over the rose petals and mix again, then seal in an airtight container. A handful of the milk bath should simply be scattered into running bathwater for a luxurious, relaxing bath.

Rose hand cream

This sweetly scented, but hard-working cream makes a very good present to give to an enthusiastic gardener whose hands are dry from weekends spent in the garden. Makes approx. 11oz.

1/2 cup sweet almond or jojoba oil
4 tablespoons shea butter
2 tablespoons beeswax, grated
1/2 cup rose water
1/2 teaspoon benzoin tincture (a natural preservative)
4 drops Rose Maroc essential oil
4 drops lavender oil (optional, though it will help heal small cuts and scratches on hard-working hands)
Dark glass jar/s

Place a small heatproof bowl over a pan of barely simmering water; the bottom of the bowl should not touch the water. Put the almond or jojoba oil into the bowl with the butter and beeswax. Warm, stirring occasionally, until the wax has melted. Leave to cool to room temperature.

Whisk together the rose water, benzoin tincture, and essential oil/s in a bowl. When the oil/wax mixture is cool, spoon it into a food processor or blender and process for a minute. With the motor still running, pour the rose water through the feed tube and process until you have a smooth emulsion. Use a spatula to transfer the cream into cold, sterilized jars and seal. This cream will keep in the refrigerator for 3–4 weeks.

Rose petal pistachio meringues

The combination of pistachios and roses gives a rather Middle Eastern twist to this most English of desserts. This recipe is a very good way of using the Rose Petal Sugar on page 98. If you're giving the meringues to an avid cook, tuck a jar of the infused sugar in the box too, so the recipient can make their own. Makes approx. 8 medium-sized meringues.

4 egg whites, at room temperature
1¼ cups rose petal sugar (page 98)
1 teaspoon rose water
½ cup shelled, unsalted pistachios, roughly chopped

Before making your meringues, make sure the bowl and whisk or beaters are scrupulously clean. Line a baking sheet with nonstick parchment paper and preheat the oven to 300°F.

Beat the egg whites until stiff. Add the rose petal sugar one spoonful at a time, beating well after each addition, until all of the sugar is used up and the mixture is stiff and glossy. Trickle the rose water and scatter two thirds of the pistachios over the top and quickly and lightly fold in with a metal spoon.

Spoon the mixture onto the prepared baking sheet in generous dollops. Scatter the remaining pistachios over the meringues. Place in the oven and immediately turn the oven down to 225°F. Bake the meringues for 1¼ hours, until you can lift them up from the parchment paper without them sticking. Turn off the oven and leave the meringues in the oven to dry out as the temperature cools.

The meringues will keep in an airtight container for 3–4 days.

PACKAGING IDEA If you're baking these in summer when the roses in your garden are abundant, make up a bouquet of your best blooms to go with the box of meringues. It makes a charming gift because home-grown roses are so much more enchanting than bought specimens.

HOW TO PLANT BARE-ROOTED ROSES

If you can, always buy bare-rooted roses. They are more economical and you often have a much wider choice of varieties. They're available by mail order and should be planted as soon as you get them. Soak them in a bucket of water for an hour before planting. Dig a hole about the width and depth of your spade. Fork in some fertilizer, such as one designed for roses, according to the package instructions. Place the rose in the hole, spreading out the roots. Lie a bamboo cane across the top of the hole and make sure the base of the stems are 1in below soil level. Back-fill with the soil you've dug out of the hole and gently heel the rose in with your foot. Water and mulch around the base. Prune the stems back to an outward-facing bud about 6in from the ground.

Rosehip jelly

This deliciously tangy and unusual jelly is very good on toast or biscuits, combined with some cream cheese or butter. Or stir into the pan juices of roast pork, venison, or duck to make a quick gravy. Makes approx. 6 x 8oz jars.

5½ cups rosehips, picked over to remove any leaves
Approx. 3lbs cooking apples
Approx. 2lbs granulated sugar
Juice of 1 lemon
Jars

Preserving pan or other large, nonreactive pan
Jelly bags or muslin
Kitchen string

Put the rosehips in a food processor and pulse a few times to break them up. Put them into the pan with 1 cup of water. Gently bring to a boil, partially cover, and simmer until the hips are very soft, about 45 minutes to an hour. Place in a jelly bag and leave to drip over a large bowl overnight. If you don't have a jelly bag, place a colander over a bowl, line it with muslin, spoon the rosehips into it, tie up with kitchen string, and suspend over the bowl. Don't be tempted to squeeze the bag or the jelly will be cloudy.

Roughly chop the cooking apples without peeling or coring them and place them in the pan with just enough water to cover. Cook gently until they form a soft and fluffy purée, about 45 minutes to an hour. Strain as for the rosehip juice. If you don't have enough muslin or jelly bags to do this simultaneously, you can do it over the course of 2 days, refrigerating the rosehip juice until the apple juice is ready.

Put two saucers in the freezer to chill. Combine the rosehip and apple juices and measure. For every 2 cups liquid, weigh out 1lb sugar. Put the fruit juices, sugar, and lemon juice into the preserving pan and warm over low heat, stirring until the sugar has dissolved. Raise the heat and boil hard until the setting point is reached. You can check this by dropping a teaspoonful of the jam onto a chilled saucer and leaving for a minute. If it wrinkles when you push it with your finger, it's ready. Remove from the heat, skim off any scum with a slotted spoon, pour into warm, sterilized jars, and seal. The jelly will keep in a cool, dark place for up to 2 months.

Scented sugars

Sugar absorbs the sweet scents of petals, leaves, and herbs beautifully and can be used to impart a subtle aroma to baking, fruity desserts, ice creams, jams, teas, and custards. A selection of scented sugars is a pretty and useful gift for an avid baker. Makes 1 cup.

FOR EACH BATCH
1 cup superfine sugar

PLUS ONE OF THE FOLLOWING INGREDIENTS
2 tablespoons lavender flowers
A small handful of rose petals
12–16 lemon verbena leaves
12–16 mint leaves
6–8 scented pelargonium leaves
Jars

Mortar and pestle (optional)

Combine the sugar with your chosen seasoning. Bash them together gently in a mortar and pestle or pulse them a couple of times in a food processor to help release the scent. Tip into a jar and seal. Leave for at least a couple of weeks for the flavors to develop and sift before using.

BEST ROSES FOR ROSEHIPS
On country walks, gather the hips from wild dog roses, *Rosa canina*. Alternatively, plant your own *R. canina*, or one of its hybrids, or one of the old *R. rugosa* varieties, all of which have beautiful rosehips in the fall.

Marigold cheese

Infusing milk with marigold petals creates a simple curd cheese with a beautiful golden color. It's very good crumbled into salads or spooned onto crackers. You must ensure that the milk you use to make it is either raw (available from some farmers' markets) or unhomogenized, which means a thick layer of cream will rise to the top of the bottle. Makes approx. 14oz.

2 quarts whole organic milk, raw or unhomogenized
2 tablespons dried marigold petals
Pinch of salt
2 teaspoons rennet, available online,
 in healthfood stores, and some supermarkets

Thermometer (optional)
Muslin

GROWING MARIGOLDS

Marigolds, *Calendula officinalis*, are a great addition to any sunny border and are as easy to grow as they are cheering to look at. They do very well in containers, hence their common name, pot marigolds. In spring, sow the seeds directly into the ground about 10in apart—ideally in rich, well-drained soil, though they seem to grow fairly contentedly almost anywhere. Dead head regularly during the summer to encourage more flowers, but be sure to leave some toward the end of the season so that they can self-seed and supply you with an abundance of pretty petals the following year. The petals have a wide range of culinary and medicinal uses and the young leaves can also be added to salads.

Pour the milk into a stainless-steel saucepan and add the marigold petals and salt. Heat the milk gently to 100°F, or blood temperature. If you don't have a thermometer, you can test this by putting your finger into the milk—it should feel neither hot nor cold. Remove the pan from the heat, stir in the rennet, and leave for about 15 minutes. The milk will separate, with the curds rising to the top and the whey remaining at the bottom of the pan.

Line a large sieve or colander with a double layer of muslin. Using a slotted spoon, gently skim off the curds and place them in the muslin. Then tie up the corners and hang the cheese to drip above a bowl or the sink for about 3 hours. If you prefer, you can leave it for up to 24 hours, which will result in a harder cheese. Unwrap the cheese, place it in a bowl, cover, and store in the fridge.

Refrigerated, the cheese will keep for about 3 days.

PACKAGING IDEA This simple cheese is the perfect thing to take along to an informal summer lunch or dinner. To transport it, wrap it in a clean circle of muslin and pack it into a small basket. A little bouquet of freshly picked marigolds makes a charming accompaniment too—they can be used to decorate the table or the fresh petals can be scattered in a pretty salad with the crumbled cheese.

Marigold, honey, and oatmeal soap

Soap making can be just as satisfying and addictive as creating delicious recipes. Combine ingredients to suit your mood, whether you want something to uplift, energize, or promote relaxation. This is a pretty and soothing concoction. Marigolds are a natural anti-inflammatory, honey nourishes and moisturizes the skin, and oatmeal is a gentle exfoliant. Cheering, soothing, citrus-based essential oils provide the perfect seasoning. Makes 10 x 2oz soaps.

18oz melt-and-mold white soap
3 tablespoons honey
5 tablespoons dried marigold petals
4 tablespoons coarse oatmeal
10 drops bergamot, neroli, or mandarin essential oil
1 tablespoon sweet almond or peanut oil
Soap molds, muffin pans, or small tart pans

Grate the soap with the coarse side of a box grater and place it in a heatproof bowl large enough to fit over one of your pans. Alternatively, you can use a double boiler. Add the honey to the soap. Place the bowl over a pan of barely simmering water—the water should not touch the bottom of the bowl—and melt the soap with the honey, stirring from time to time, until it's liquid and well blended.

Remove the bowl from the heat. Stir in the marigold petals, oatmeal, and essential oils and mix thoroughly. Lightly but thoroughly grease the molds with a little of the sweet almond or peanut oil. Pour the liquid soap into a measuring cup and then pour it into the molds. Rap the molds gently on the work surface to eliminate air bubbles (this isn't necessary if you are using silicone molds) and leave to set for at least 4 hours.

If you're using silicone molds, simply press the soaps out. If using metal molds, use a small, sharp knife to help ease them out. Leave in a cool, dry place for 3–4 weeks to "cure" or harden.

DRYING MARIGOLD PETALS

Pick the marigolds (*Calendula officinalis*) when the flowers are fully open, on a sunny morning after the dew has evaporated. Place them on a drying screen (page 90) in a dry, shady, well-ventilated place and turn them regularly until they are papery. Pull the petals from the buds and store them in a dark glass jar or other opaque container until ready to use. As well as using them to add color to simple cheeses (page 100), you can infuse them in tea (page 57), scatter them over risottos or pilafs, or use them in beauty preparations such as the Marigold Face Tonic (page 105).

PACKAGING
New or vintage muffin and tart pans in interesting shapes make great soap molds. You can simply unmold the soaps and pack them in a pretty box or give them in the pans, as an extra little gift for the lucky recipient.

Marigold face tonic

Marigold petals have natural antiseptic properties and have been used in preparations to promote clear complexions for centuries. This mild toner is suitable for all skin types. Makes approx. 2½ cups.

1 tablespoon dried marigold petals
Approx. 1 cup witch hazel
4 tablespoons rose water
2 tablespoons glycerine
1 teaspoon benzoin tincture
    (natural preservative)

Muslin
Funnel
Pretty bottles, ideally made from
    dark glass

Place the marigold petals in a glass or ceramic bowl and pour over 1⅔ cups boiling water. Cover and leave the mixture to infuse for 3–4 hours. Strain the infusion through a sieve lined with muslin into a bowl. Measure and stir in an equal amount of witch hazel, followed by the rose water, glycerine, and benzoin tincture. Use a funnel to decant into cold, sterilized bottles.

The tonic will keep for up to a month, or 2 months if stored in the fridge.

TYPES OF MARIGOLDS

The kind of marigolds used in cooking and beauty preparations are *Calendula officinalis*, or pot marigolds, which are renowned for their antiseptic and soothing properties. Don't confuse them with *Tagetes*, more commonly called French or African marigolds. *Tagetes* petals are inedible, but consider planting some anyway as they're among the most useful of all the companion plants. Their roots give off a powerful aroma that deters harmful nematodes and slugs and, planted near tomatoes, they are believed to discourage whitefly.

Sage water skin tonic

Sage is an excellent antiseptic and is very effective at combating oily skin, making this a particularly good gift for a teenager prone to blemishes. Makes approx. 1 cup.

1 tablespoon fresh sage leaves
2 tablespoons cider vinegar
1 teaspoon glycerine
¼ teaspoon benzoin tincture
    (a natural preservative)
Dark glass 8oz bottle

Muslin or paper coffee filter
Small funnel

Bring some water to a boil and place the sage leaves in a heatproof bowl, crushing them lightly with your hands to help release their scent. Pour over 1 cup of boiling water, cover, and leave to steep for 20 minutes.

Place a sieve over a bowl and line with muslin or a paper coffee filter. Strain the sage infusion, pressing down with the back of a spoon to extract as much of the sage liquid as possible. Whisk in the vinegar and glycerine and pour through a funnel into a cold, sterilized bottle. Seal and refrigerate.

The tonic should be applied to the skin on a cotton pad twice a day after cleansing.

This tonic will keep in the refrigerator for a week.

Teacup planters

Single teacups can be picked up fairly inexpensively at supermarkets, thrift stores, and yard sales. They make perfect, pretty planters for small flowers, foliage, and bulbs. You could also use sugar bowls or small milk pitchers or teapots. Because of their scale, teacup planters look particularly good on bedside tables, on desks, or by the bathtub, where their patterns, colors, textures, and scents can be peacefully enjoyed.

SOME SUGGESTIONS FOR TEACUP PLANTERS

Crocuses
Daisies (*Bellis perennis*)
Dwarf cyclamen
Dwarf irises
Lily of the valley
Miniature daffodils, such as
   'Tête à Tête'
Primroses
Small-leaved ivies
Small sempervivums
Snowdrops
Violets

Cup and saucer, or other
   small container
Small gravel, for drainage
Potting soil

Masking tape
Dish towel
Protective goggles
Power drill and small
   ceramic tile bit

To transform your teacup into a planter, you are first going to need to add some drainage. To do this, place a small strip of masking tape in the middle of the interior base of the cup. Turn the cup upside down on a board covered in a dish towel. The board will protect the work surface from the drill bit and the dish towel will stop the cup from moving around. Place some masking tape on the middle of the cup's upturned base and mark the center of the base with an "X." Put on your goggles and, using the ceramic tile bit, slowly drill a hole in the bottom of the teacup. Remove the tape.

Place a thin layer of gravel in the bottom of the teacup and scatter on some soil. Pot your chosen plant, firm it in gently, and water. Once the plant has finished flowering, either discard or plant outside where it may come back the following year.

GROWING GRAPE HYACINTHS

In the middle of winter, the delicate scent and intensely blue flower spikes of grape hyacinths, *Muscari*, are positively heart-warming. Little pots or planters of them dotted around the house promise that spring is imminent.

GROWING BULBS IN TEACUPS

In fall, scatter some potting soil in your planter (for grape hyacinths, choose a teacup about 3in deep), then set the bulbs side by side on top, allowing one to three bulbs per cup depending on its size—their tips should be level with the rim of the cup. Scatter some more potting soil over the top and water sparingly. Next, you need to place the bulbs in a cold (about 40°F), dark shed or cellar for several weeks, ensuring that the soil is kept barely moist, until shoots appear. This can take 8–10 weeks. Once the shoots appear, bring into the house and water. If you keep the planter in a coolish part of the house and away from strong direct sunlight, the flowers should last 3–4 weeks.

Bath fizzies

You can customize these bath fizzies with dried herbs, flowers, and essential oils according to your mood or the person you're giving them to. Chamomile creates a relaxing bath, whereas jasmine is sensual and uplifting. Bath bomb molds are available from some craft stores and online, but you can also use large silicone ice-cube trays or muffin pans. Makes 6-8, depending on the size of the mold.

10½oz baking soda
5½oz citric acid, available online
5 tablespoons dried chamomile or dried
  jasmine flowers
12 drops chamomile or jasmine essential oil
Witch hazel

Spray bottle
Bath bomb molds or large silicone ice-cube trays
  or muffin pans

Sift together the baking soda and citric acid several times until everything is well blended. Mix in the dried flowers and sprinkle over the essential oil.

Spray on some witch hazel, stirring the mixture with your other hand as you spray. You need to spray just enough witch hazel to get your fizzies to stick together, but not so much that they start to react and fizz. As soon as the mixture holds together like damp sand when you squeeze it in your hands, place it in your molds, packing it in quite tightly to ensure a sturdy bath fizzy.

Leave the mixture to set in the molds for an hour, then turn out onto parchment paper and leave to harden for a few hours or overnight.

The bath fizzies will keep for several months in an airtight container.

GROWING JASMINE

Considering its delicate appearance and heady, exotic scent, jasmine is surprisingly undemanding to grow. Winter-flowering jasmine, *Jasminum nudiflorum*, produces starry, yellow blossoms on its naked stems when little else is in flower, but for scent you really want its summer cousin, *J. officinale*. This deciduous climber needs a warm, sunny site to flourish and will clamber over trellises and pergolas, though it will need the support of wires to grow up against a house wall. Water freely in spring and summer, and prune after flowering to maintain its shape.

PACKAGING IDEA
Wrap the bath fizzies in clear cellophane and tie them with ribbon. Pack several in a basket with other bathtime treats such as the Fennel & Honey Face Mask (page 162) or Cornflower Eye Compresses (page 118).

Almond and lemon-scented geranium cookies

Using scented sugar gives these simple almond cookies a more complex and intriguing flavor. If your sweet-toothed recipient is a plant lover too, a pretty pot containing a scented pelargonium (geranium) along with the batch of cookies makes a great gift. Makes approx. 20.

7 tablespoons unsalted butter, softened
5 tablespoons lemon-scented pelargonium sugar
   (page 98), sifted
1 cup self-rising flour, sifted
1oz ground almonds
2 small lemon-scented pelargonium leaves,
   finely shredded
Grated zest of $\frac{1}{2}$ small lemon
1–2 tablespoons milk
Approx. 20 whole, blanched almonds

Preheat the oven to 350°F. Line two baking sheets with parchment paper.

Cream together the butter and sugar until light and fluffy. Beat in the flour, ground almonds, pelargonium leaves, lemon zest, and just enough milk to make a firm dough. Shape into walnut-sized balls and arrange on the baking sheets, leaving about 1in of space between each cookie because they spread out while they're cooking. Slightly flatten the balls and press a whole almond into the top of each one.

Bake the cookies for about 10–12 minutes until lightly golden around the edges. Allow to cool on the sheets for a couple of minutes before placing on a wire rack to cool completely.

The cookies will keep in an airtight tin for 3–4 days.

PELARGONIUM VARIETIES

Use this recipe as a starting point and vary the flavor of the cookies by infusing the sugar with different scented pelargoniums. Some good ones are:

CITRUSY
P. 'Mabel Grey', *P.* 'Prince of Orange', *P.* 'Lemon Fancy'

ROSE-SCENTED
P. graveolens, *P.* 'Attar of Roses'

SPICY
P. 'Fragrans' (nutmeg)

MINTY
P. tomentosum

PACKAGING IDEA

If you're giving the cookies to an avid baker, tuck a jar of the scented sugar into the package, too.

Moth-banishing pelargoniums

There are few more annoying wardrobe problems than unfolding a favorite sweater and finding it has been nibbled by moths. Worse, they really seem to love the good stuff, tucking into cashmere, silk, and linen while leaving cheaper, synthetic clothes untouched. If you have a fashionable friend, a moth-banishing scented pelargonium makes a natural, enduring, and practical gift. Add a card with instructions on drying the leaves and perhaps some Moth-repellent Sachets (page 35) to get them started.

1 scented pelargonium (see list)
Pretty pot

There are hundreds of varieties of scented pelargoniums, but for the purposes of this present, the most heavily scented ones work best. The dried leaves can be sewn or tucked into sachets (page 31) and placed in closets or drawers, where their strong smell will deter moths from planting their damaging little eggs. They hunt out fabric by scent, so baffling them with pelargoniums is highly effective.

The best part of giving a friend a living plant is that when the dried leaves lose their potency, they can simply pluck a few more. This benefits the pelargonium too, as it promotes stronger, thicker growth. It really is a houseplant which earns its keep.

BEST MOTH-BANISHING VARIETIES

The following pelargonium varieties make wonderful houseplants, releasing their scent and freshening the air as you brush past them, but their strong scents are less popular with hungry pests. They are believed to deter mosquitoes too, which makes an even more compelling reason to give one a home.

CITRUSY
'Prince of Orange', 'Orange Fizz', 'Bitter Lemon', 'Queen of the Lemons'

ROSE-SCENTED
'Lady Plymouth', 'Vandersea', 'Attar of Roses', 'Rober's Lemon Rose'

CEDAR-SCENTED
'Painted Lady', 'Clorinda', 'Copthorne', 'Souvenir de Prue'

GROWING PELARGONIUMS

Pelargoniums make very good houseplants, but if you can give them a little vacation outdoors for a few weeks in the summer, it will improve their vigor. Indoors, place the plant in a bright spot where it will receive some direct sunlight for part of the day. In spring and summer, water generously enough that water comes through the drainage holes of the pot but allow the surface of the soil to dry out between watering. Feed once every couple of weeks with a diluted high-potash plant food, such as tomato fertilizer, and take the chance to pick over the plant, removing any dead leaves and fading blooms. In fall, cut the plant back by half to encourage bushy growth and reduce watering, keeping the soil almost dry through the winter until the plant starts to show signs of new growth the following spring.

Scented room spray

Capture the scents of your garden at high summer in a bottle. Makes approx. 1 cup.

1 tablespoon fresh rose petals
1 tablespoon fresh scented pelargonium leaves
2 teaspoons fresh lemon verbena leaves
1 teaspoon fresh lemon thyme leaves
1 tablespoon fresh lavender leaves and flowers
$^{1}/_{2}$ cup orange blossom water or rose water
4 drops each orange, rose, and lavender essential oil
1 teaspoon benzoin tincture (a natural preservative)
Pretty spray bottles

Muslin
Funnel

Combine the petals, leaves, and flowers with 2 cups water and simmer for 15 minutes. Leave to steep, covered, overnight.

Line a sieve with muslin and strain the infused water. Then, in a bowl, whisk together with the orange blossom or rose water, essential oils, and benzoin tincture. Use a funnel to decant into cold, sterilized spray bottles.

The spray will keep for about 2 months, up to 4 months if refrigerated.

PROPAGATING PELARGONIUMS FROM CUTTINGS

There are so many varieties of scented pelargoniums that collecting them can become quite addictive. It's fortunate, then, that they're so simple to propagate from cuttings, which makes them very easy to swap and share with friends. In late summer, take a cutting about 4in long, cutting just below a leaf joint, and strip the leaves from the lower part with a sharp knife, leaving only two or three leaves at the top of the stem. Fill a 3in pot with a mixture of equal parts seed compost and either fine chipped bark or pea gravel. Make four to six holes 1in deep around the edge of the pot and insert the cuttings. Gently firm them in and water lightly. Place the pot in a warm place out of direct sunlight until they root. Water sparingly while the cuttings take and pot them on once new leaves start to grow.

Pansies in cheese boxes

When I buy soft cheeses, they often come in such pretty wooden boxes I'm reluctant to throw them away. I put them to use as unusual temporary planters for small flowers, such as pansies. They make simple, inexpensive table decorations, which I then give away to guests. The small, wooden containers that gourmet French butter is sometimes packed in also make very good containers for small plants. If you follow the Victorian language of flowers, pansies are a particularly appropriate gift to give to your friends as they mean "loving thoughts." The word pansy derives from the French word pensée, or thought, because their dainty flowers look so much like human faces.

A selection of wooden cheese boxes or
    butter containers (different ones look
    better if giving to several guests)
Plastic wrap
Potting soil
Pansies, or other small flowering plants
Moss (optional)

Line the cheese boxes with plastic wrap and partially fill them with potting soil. Remove the pansies from their pots and gently transplant them into the boxes. Water very lightly. If you like, you can cover the soil surrounding the pansies with moss.

Obviously, the plants won't thrive in these conditions for long, but you and your guests can enjoy them for a few days before planting them out in the garden.

GROWING PANSIES

Pansies, *Viola* x *wittrockiana*, those most cheerful of cottage garden plants, are always a happy sight in the garden, tilting their sweet faces towards the sun. They can be tricky to germinate (though will enthusiastically self-seed once in the garden), but nurseries usually carry such a wide range at relatively low cost, it hardly seems worth the trouble. Enjoy them through the spring, deadheading to encourage more flowers and cutting back when they start to set seed. You may get a second flush of flowers in the autumn.

Cornflower eye compresses

For centuries, infusions of cornflowers have been used to soothe tired and irritated eyes. These cornflower compresses would be a thoughtful gift for a friend who spends long hours at a computer screen, or whose eyes are sore from hayfever or a long flight.

Makes 10, enough for 5 treatments.

Approx. 1½oz dried cornflower petals
  (see page 100 for instructions on drying petals)
Muslin
Sewing machine or needle and thread

Cut out the muslin into 20 circles approximately 3in in diameter. Pin two circles together and stitch about ½in in from the edge, leaving a gap of about ¾in in the stitching. Spoon a teaspoon of the dried petals into the circle and sew it closed. Repeat with the rest of the circles.

To use the compresses, place two of them in a small bowl and pour over just enough boiling water to cover. Leave to steep in the liquid until cold. Lie back, place a circle on each eye and relax for 10 minutes. Discard the circles after using.

PACKAGING IDEA Tie the circles together in a bundle with ribbon and place in a pretty box, along with the instructions on how to use the compresses on a label or card. Perhaps add a packet of cornflower seeds too—they're so easy to grow and so striking in the flower bed, it would be difficult to think of anyone who wouldn't love them.

GROWING CORNFLOWERS

Cornflowers, *Centaurea cyanus*, like to grow in well-drained soil in full sun. Sow straight into the ground, in either the fall or spring, or both if you want to guarantee a long succession of flowers from late spring through the summer. Prepare the soil by raking it over and removing any weeds or stones. Scatter the seeds sparingly and rake them in before giving the area a good water. When the seedlings appear, thin them to about 12in apart. Keep cutting at the flowers to encourage more blooms. Cornflowers make excellent cut flowers and will last in a vase in the house for a week or more.

CORNFLOWER

Field

Pinecone garland

If you have a friend whose festive taste leans more toward the natural than the tinsel, this garland is a beautiful gift which will last for many years. Collect pinecones from the garden or on winter walks, and supplement your bounty with cones bought from garden centers, craft stores, or suppliers online.

Paper-covered wire, available from garden centers and suppliers
A large quantity of small pinecones, at least 100
Jute garden string
Dried orange slices (see page 123), optional
Dried apple slices (see page 123), optional
Bay leaves, optional

Large needle, if you're adding orange slices and bay leaves

Cut the wire into 4in lengths and wrap a length tightly around the base of each cone, concealing the wire in the microsporophylls (that's "leaves" to you and me) of the cone. Begin tying the cones into the garden string. Tie them in tightly, bunching them up together, so the string is well covered. Trim off the excess wire. If you're interspersing the cones with orange and apple slices and bay leaves, thread the string on the large needle and poke it through the slices and bay leaves. Small bundles of each look better than single specimens.

When you have the length you want, tie a loop at each end of the string to attach the garland to a fireplace, doorframe, or stair banister.

Pinecone firelighters

A bag of these makes a fantastic seasonal gift for any friend who has an open fire. They look beautiful coated simply with the beeswax, but you can color them red and green by grating a couple of wax crayons in with the wax, if you like. The essential oils are optional but add a lovely seasonal scent. Makes 12.

12 small pinecones
12 paper muffin cases
Waxed wicks or garden string
About 1¹/₂lb wax, either beeswax or paraffin wax
Wax crayons, grated (optional)
Essential oils, e.g. orange, cedar, sandalwood, clove, nutmeg, pine (alone or in combination—optional)

Double boiler, or a heatproof bowl you can fit over one of your pans
Small muffin pan

If you've gathered your own pinecones and they feel a little damp, place them on a baking sheet and dry them out in the oven at 350°F for 10–15 minutes.

Line the muffin tray with the paper cases. Tie a length of wick or string around the base of each cone, leaving a tail of about 3in.

Gently melt the wax (and the grated crayons, if you want colored wax) in a double boiler or in a heatproof bowl over a pan of simmering water. Don't leave unattended at any point while melting.

When the wax has melted, stir in any essential oils if you're using them. Hang the cones upside down by the wicks and dip them in the wax, making sure you dip some of the wick to. Place them in the center of the muffin cases, draping the wicks over the sides. Carefully pour or ladle the wax into the muffin cases around the cones, letting it come about half-way up each case. Leave to cool and set.

Tuck a pinecone firelighter in among the kindling before lighting the fire.

Frosted holly leaves

"Frosting" the edge of holly leaves is an easy project that small children might like to help you with. Use the leaves to adorn wreaths (page 123), decorate Christmas wrapping (page 14), or as part of a Christmas flower arrangement. You may well have Epsom salts left over from some of the other projects in this book—they look more natural and subtle than glitter.

Holly sprigs
Glue pen or clear craft glue
Epsom salts

Fill a bowl with Epsom salts. Working with one holly sprig at a time, paint a thin layer of glue around the edges of the leaves. Hold the sprig over the bowl and use a teaspoon to dredge the leaves with the Epsom salts. Place on a wire rack to dry. Continue with the rest of the sprigs.

Christmas wreath

Making your own wreath is guaranteed to get you into the Christmas spirit. It's very simple to do and the results are impressive. I like to use highly scented things to decorate my wreath, such as lemons, cloves, and cinnamon, which give a delicious waft of Christmas as you enter the house. Makes 1.

FOR THE WREATH

1 flat-wire wreath, approx. diameter 12–16in, available from florists, suppliers online, or some garden centers

Moss, available from garden centers or florists

Florist's wire, thick and fine gauges

A selection of thin ribbon for tying bundles and wide ribbon for hanging the wreath

TO DECORATE

A selection of: apples, berries, cinnamon sticks, cloves, fir branches (which can be off-cuts from your Christmas tree), eucalyptus, ivy, lemons and/or limes, oranges, pinecones, star anise

Garden shears
Needle and thread
Glue gun, or some strong glue
Staple gun or tacks

First, make the dried orange or apple slices, if you are planning to use them. Slice the fruit very thinly and dry on wire racks in the oven on its lowest setting for several hours or overnight.

To assemble the wreath, begin by covering the wire form generously with moss, then tie it securely using thick florist's wire. Next, tie in sprigs of fir and/or eucalyptus so that the wreath is densely covered. Then wind ivy around the wreath, securing it at intervals with fine florist's wire.

You can use the dried apple and orange slices singly or glued together in stacks of three. Cut a length of fine florist's wire approximately 8in long and push it through the center of the apple or orange slice/s, then push it back through about 1/2in from the original hole—this will give you a loop of wire to tie the slice/s to the wreath. Cover the wire on the front of the slice/s by gluing on a star anise.

Glue together bundles of cinnamon sticks and wind around a length of fine wire to attach them to the wreath. Cover the wire with ribbon and tie it into a bow. Stud the lemons or limes with cloves and push a length of thick wire through the center of each, long enough to tie it to the wreath.

Tie lengths of fine wire to the pinecones, berry sprigs, and anything else you want to include. Lay it flat on a table and arrange the various elements around it until you have an arrangement you like, leaving space for the ribbon you're going to use to attach it to the door. Tie in your decorations securely, hiding any pieces of wire beneath the fir and ivy. Attach a loop of ribbon at the center-top of the wreath and sew it on securely, leaving enough of a "tail" to attach it to the door. Hide the stitches with a generous bow. Use staples or tacks to attach the length of ribbon to the top of the door.

GROWING IVY

Ivy, *Hedera*, is a garden workhorse. It grows in tough places where more refined plants struggle and comes in many varieties, from dainty to bold, rich green, to variegated and golden. In winter it provides a welcome splash of lush color and sometimes berries, invaluable to birds and insects. Ivies can be grown up walls, trained over tree stumps, or in pots or hanging baskets. Generally, the *Hedera* genus prefers a limy soil, so add a handful of lime to the planting hole. Yellow varieties do best in a sunny spot; green or silver varieties do well in shade or sun.

FRUIT, VEGETABLES & NUTS

Crème de cassis

This luscious liqueur is traditionally served with white wine as a kir or with champagne as a kir royale, but it's also delicious poured over very good vanilla ice cream to create a near-instant dessert. Crème de cassis, made in the summer and allowed to mature for a few months, makes a very good Christmas present. Makes approx. 7 cups.

1½lbs black currants, picked over to remove any stalks
3 cups red wine
Approx. 2lbs superfine sugar
Approx. 1½ cups vodka
Pretty bottles

Muslin
Funnel

Place the black currants in a ceramic or glass bowl and mash lightly with a potato masher. Stir in the red wine, cover with plastic wrap, and leave to macerate for at least 24 and up to 48 hours.

Purée the black currants and wine in a food processor or blender and then strain through a muslin-lined sieve into a bowl. Press down on the fruit with a wooden spoon to extract as much juice as possible. Measure the volume of liquid (you should have about 1 quart), then pour it into a large saucepan. For every cup of liquid, add 3½ cups superfine sugar.

Heat gently, stirring frequently, until the sugar has dissolved. Do not let the liquid simmer, as you don't want to boil off the alcohol. Leave the mixture barely steaming at the lowest heat for an hour or so, stirring occasionally, until the liquid has reduced and become slightly syrupy—you should have about 5 cups. Leave to cool.

Mix together 1 part vodka to 3 parts of the cooled black currant liquid. Use a funnel to decant into cold, sterilized bottles. Store in a cool, dark place for at least a month before drinking.

The crème de cassis should be drunk within 2 years.

GROWING BLACK CURRANTS

Black currants, *Ribes nigrum*, are generous croppers—a happy, established bush can provide up to 10lbs of fruit each year. Plant in fertile, acidic, well-drained soil in as sunny a spot as you can muster, though they will tolerate some shade. Ideally, plant your black currant bush in late fall or winter and, a couple of weeks before planting, dig some well-rotted compost into the soil. Dig a hole twice as big as the root ball, tease out the roots if you're planting a container-grown specimen, back-fill and firm the bush in well. Mulch with a layer of bark or compost to help prevent moisture loss. In the first spring after planting, chop down the stems to two buds above ground level to encourage the growth of new stems.

Red currant & rose syrup

This makes a delightful gift to take along to a summer party. It's delicious diluted with champagne or over ice with soda water, and if any remains the next morning, your hosts can trickle it over pancakes at breakfast. Makes 3 x 25oz bottles.

A handful of rose petals (see page 90 for highly scented varieties)
12oz fruity rosé wine
3¹/₃lbs red currants
Approx. 4 cups Rose Petal Sugar (page 98), sifted
Bottles

Preserving pan or large, nonreactive saucepan
Jelly bag or muslin
Kitchen string
Funnel

Place the rose petals in a pan with the rosé wine. Bring to a simmer, remove from the heat, and leave to infuse for 2 hours. Strain into a bowl.

Put the red currants into a preserving pan with the infused wine and crush them a bit with a potato masher. Bring to a simmer, cover, and cook for 30 minutes until the currants are very soft. Remove from the heat and crush again. Spoon the mixture into a jelly bag over a bowl. Alternatively line a colander with muslin, place over a bowl, and spoon the currants into the center; tie up with kitchen string and suspend over the bowl. Leave to drip overnight.

Measure the juice. For every 2 cups of juice, weigh out 2 cups of rose petal sugar. Put the juice and sugar back into the preserving pan and warm over medium heat, stirring to dissolve the sugar. When the sugar has dissolved, boil hard for 5 minutes or until sufficiently syrupy. Remove from the heat and skim off any scum with a slotted spoon. Decant into warm, sterilized bottles and seal.

The syrup will keep in the fridge for up to a month.

Growing Red Currants

Red currants, or *Ribes rubrum*, are self-fertile, so you only need one bush to produce a crop. They do best in good, well-drained soil in a sheltered position where they'll receive plenty of sun, but they are remarkably tolerant of less-than-ideal conditions. Mulch in spring with a layer of well-rotted compost, potting soil, or straw. Water regularly in the growing season, until you've finished harvesting the fruit, and keep the ground around the bush as weed-free as possible.

Red currants bear their fruit on old wood. Prune in late winter just before the buds begin to swell. Cut back any very old branches to ground level, then prune back new growth to two buds in early summer to keep the bush compact. When the beautiful, jewellike strings of fruit are ripe, cut whole trusses and use them as quickly as possible as they do not keep well. You may need to throw a net over your bush to stop the birds and squirrels getting to the fruit before you do.

Cherries in brandy

Though a rather luxurious treat to receive, this is a very simple gift to make. A few jars prepared in summer when cherries are plentiful and sweet make great Christmas presents. The cherries can be spooned over ice cream or panna cotta, and the brandy is also very good served chilled in shot or liqueur glasses. Makes approx. 1.2 quarts.

18oz sweet or morello cherries
Approx. 3/4 cup superfine or vanilla sugar
2/3 cup brandy

OPTIONAL FLAVORINGS

A strip of orange zest, pared with a vegetable peeler and all traces of white pith removed or 1 vanilla pod, split
1.2-quart jar

Rinse the cherries and remove the stems, but leave the pits in as this makes for a better flavor and texture.

Place the cherries in a large, cold, sterilized jar, then add the sugar. If you are using morello cherries, add a tablespoon or two more of sugar to sweeten. Tuck the orange zest or vanilla pod in among the fruit, if you wish to add more flavor. Pour over the brandy. Seal the jar and shake a few times to help the sugar begin to dissolve.

Store in a cool, dark place for 2 months, shaking the jar from time to time to help the sugar dissolve.

Unopened, the cherries will keep for 6 months. After opening, store in the fridge and eat within a month.

GROWING MORELLO CHERRIES

If you have room for only one cherry tree, make it a morello. Sour cherries, *Prunus cerasus*, of which morellos are a variety, are difficult to buy in some stores and are so delicious in baking, in jams, or preserved in brandy. They are also self-fertile and, unlike sweet cherries, *Prunus avium*, which need full sun to develop their optimum sweetness, morellos do well in shady spots and grow successfully against north- or east-facing walls. As an added bonus, they're also less attractive to birds than their sweeter cousins.

Blackberry jam

Whether it's made with gathered or cultivated blackberries, this lovely jam is one of the best flavors of high summer.

Makes about 4 x 8oz jars.

1lb cooking apples, peeled, cored and diced
1lb blackberries
Juice of 1/2 lemon
3 1/2 cups granulated sugar
Jars

Preserving pan or large, nonreactive saucepan

Place two saucers in the freezer.

Put the diced apples in the preserving pan with 1/2 cup of water. Simmer gently for 10 minutes until the apples have broken up into a soft, fluffy pulp. Add the blackberries and lemon juice and continue to cook for about 5 minutes until the blackberries soften and begin to release their juices.

Add the sugar and stir over low heat until it has dissolved. Bring to a boil and boil rapidly for about 15 minutes, until the jam reaches its setting point. You can test this by spooning a little of the jam onto one of the chilled saucers and leaving it for a moment to cool. Push it with your finger, and if it wrinkles, the jam is ready. Remove from the heat and skim off any scum with a slotted spoon. Spoon into hot, sterilized jars and seal.

The jam will keep, sealed, for up to a year.

For tips on growing blackberries, see page 135.

Fruit cheeses

Fruit cheeses make a great gift for lovers of strong, hard cheeses as they go together beautifully. Use up a glut of orchard fruits or a generous haul of fruit from a blackberry walk. Makes approx. 2lbs.

FRUITS TO CHOOSE FROM

$3\frac{1}{3}$lbs plums (firm ones with some
   tartness rather than ripe dessert plums)
   or damsons, pits removed
$2\frac{1}{4}$lbs blackberries with
   1lb cooking apples, diced
1lb 10oz pears, diced, with
   1lb 10oz cooking apples, diced,
1lb quinces, diced, with
   $2\frac{1}{4}$lbs cooking apples, diced

Granulated sugar
Straight-sided jars or small dishes

Preserving pan or large, nonreactive saucepan
Nylon sieve
Glycerine
Food-grade paraffin wax, for sealing

Put the fruit into the pan with about 1 cup of water. Simmer gently over low heat until you have a soft, thick pulp. Rub through a nylon sieve, pressing with a wooden spoon to retrieve as much pulp as possible. Weigh the pulp. For every $1\frac{1}{3}$lbs pulp, weigh out 1lb of sugar.

Put the pulp and sugar into a clean pan and warm over low heat, stirring, until the sugar has dissolved. Bring to a boil, lower the heat and simmer, stirring frequently, until the mixture is very thick and glossy, about 50–60 minutes.

Brush the inside of the hot, sterilized jars with a little glycerine (this will make it easier to unmold the cheese later) and pour in the fruit cheese. Seal and store in a cool, dark place for at least a month before using. If your containers don't have lids or it's difficult to seal them using wax paper disks and cellophane covers, seal them with melted food-grade paraffin wax.

Fruit cheese will keep, unopened, for a year.

GRoWINg PLUMs

Give plums a fertile, well-drained site in full sun and plant your tree in late fall/early winter to give it a chance to establish itself before the weather warms up in spring. Some varieties are self-fertile but all do better if they have companions, so plant two if you have the space. If you have a small garden, consider one on a dwarfing rootstock, which will only reach a height of about 10ft or a fan-trained one, which will take up little space but still provide lots of tasty fruit. Keep the tree well watered until it's established and apply a thick layer of mulch in spring to help it retain precious moisture.

Fruit leathers

Making fruit leather is similar to making fruit cheese, except that once you've made your purée you bake it very slowly in the oven until it forms a pliable sheet.

For every $2\frac{1}{4}$lbs fruit you'll need
   5oz honey

Cook the fruit down with a little water until very soft, then press through a nylon sieve and stir in the honey while it's still warm. Line baking sheets with parchment paper, brush them with a little peanut oil and spread out the purée in a thin, even layer. Bake at the lowest possible oven temperature for 6–8 hours, until pliable but not sticky. Cool and then roll it up in plastic wrap or cut it into strips, roll them up and store in an airtight container.

Fruit leathers keep for 2 months in an airtight container or 4 months in the fridge.

Raspberry & scented pelargonium jam

This jam is a good way of using Scented Pelargonium Sugar (page 98), which enhances the natural sweetness of the raspberries with its own subtle aroma.

Makes approx. 6 x 8oz jars.

2$\frac{1}{4}$lbs raspberries
2$\frac{1}{4}$lbs scented pelargonium sugar (page 98),
   sifted to remove any leaves
Jars

Preserving pan or large, nonreactive saucepan

Put two saucers in the freezer.

Place the raspberries in the preserving pan and mash them roughly with a wooden spoon or potato masher. Heat very gently until the fruit is just simmering, then add the sugar. Continue to cook, stirring, on very low heat until the sugar has dissolved. Raise the temperature and boil rapidly for 10–15 minutes until the setting point is reached. You can test this by spooning a little of the jam onto one of the chilled saucers and leaving it for a moment to cool. Push it with your finger, and if it wrinkles, the jam is ready.

Remove from the heat and skim off any scum with a slotted spoon. Pot into hot, sterilized jars and seal.

The jam will keep, sealed, for up to a year.

PLANTING RASPBERRIES

When planning your raspberry beds, choose as sunny a spot as you can. Raspberries, *Rubus idaeus*, are self-fertile and pollinated by insects, so give them some protection in windy sites. Ideally, you want well-drained soil that has a neutral to slightly acidic pH value. A couple of weeks before planting, clear the soil of weeds, dig in some well-rotted compost and erect post-and-wire supports for the canes. Plant your raspberries in winter, in rows about 20in apart, allowing 6ft between rows. Cut the canes down to about 12in above the soil, pruning above a bud, and water in well. Raspberries fruit on last year's canes, so you won't get any fruit in the first summer after planting.

PACKAGING IDEA

Create an afternoon-tea basket by packing up a jar of this jam with a batch of freshly cooked scones.

Blackberry gin

This delicious, fruity gin can be enjoyed ice-cold in shot glasses, added to a glass of champagne, or poured over ice and topped up with soda water. It makes a special gift on its own, or pair it with some pretty glasses or a bottle of fizz if you're feeling generous. Makes approx. 1.4 quarts.

2¼lbs blackberries, washed and picked over

3 cups sugar

1 vanilla pod, split lengthwise with
  a small, sharp knife

1 quart gin

2 x 25oz bottles

2-quart screwtop or Kilner-type jar

Funnel

Make sure that the jar is scrupulously clean and add the blackberries and sugar in layers, tucking the vanilla pod somewhere in the middle. Pour over 3 cups of the gin, seal the lid, and shake gently. The next day, once the blackberries have settled a bit, top up with the remaining gin.

Shake the jar every day for a week to dissolve the sugar completely. Then shake once a week for about 8 weeks. Strain the liquid through a fine sieve and pour through a funnel into the bottles and seal. The boozy blackberries are delicious on ice cream, so don't discard them.

Keep the gin in a cool, dark place for 12 months before drinking if you can, though it tastes very good after as little as 3 months.

ALTERNATIVE: QUINCE VODKA

You can use the same method to make quince vodka, which takes on the deliciously perfumed flavor of the quinces and turns an elegant shade of pale amber. Simply wash any fluff from the skin of about 2lbs of quinces, then grate the skin and flesh (discarding any pips) and tip into a large jar, alternating layers of grated quince with ¾ cup of sugar. You could also add a couple of star anise, a cinnamon stick, or a split vanilla pod to the jar before topping up with about 1½ quarts of vodka.

GROWING BLACKBERRIES

Gathering a basket of juicy blackberries, *Rubus fruticosus*, along the hedgerows is one of the joys of late summer. But if you have space, it's simple to establish your own patch. They're the easiest of berries to grow, tolerating fairly poor soil and some shade with fruity good humor. Many cultivated varieties have the advantage of being thornless and tend to be plumper and sweeter than wild ones too. All blackberries are self-fertile. Plant them in the fall, digging plenty of well-rotted compost or organic matter into the planting hole, and mulch in spring. Water during dry spells in the growing season and cut back fruiting stems after harvesting to allow for new growth. Blackberries can be fan-trained up a wall or fence, which makes picking even easier.

Quince jellies

These jewellike sweets in a rich shade of amber are a delicious way to end a meal. Take a box of them along to a dinner party as a fruity alternative to chocolates.

Makes about 40 jellies.

Approx. 2¼lbs quinces
2 strips of lemon peel, pared
  with a sharp vegetable peeler
  and all white pith removed
Approx. 3½ cups granulated
  sugar, plus extra for coating
  the jellies
A little vegetable oil,
  for greasing
Baking sheet, approx.
  12 x 8 x 1in

Wash the quinces to remove any of the fluffy coating on the skin. Chop roughly, without peeling or coring. Put the quinces in a large pan with the lemon zest and add just enough water to cover. Bring to a simmer and cook until soft and pulpy. Cover and leave overnight.

Rub the quinces through a sieve. Weigh the purée and return it to a large, clean pan with an equal weight of sugar. Warm gently, stirring until the sugar has dissolved. Bring to a gentle boil and cook, stirring frequently, until the mixture is thick, stiff and glossy. This can take up to 1½ hours. The jelly is ready when, if you draw a wooden spoon through the middle, the bottom of the pan is visible for a second before the mixture comes back together.

Line the baking sheet with parchment paper and brush lightly with oil. Pour the mixture into the baking sheet and leave overnight in a cool, dry place to set. Once it is set, turn the mixture out onto a sheet of parchment paper and cut into jellies. Toss in granulated sugar to coat.

Stored in an airtight container with waxed paper between the layers, the jellies will keep for up to a month.

GROWING QUINCES

Quince, *Cydonia oblonga*, are self-fertile and relatively low-maintenance. They make a beautiful addition to any garden and are enormously useful in the kitchen. Plant quinces in late fall before the first frosts in rich, moist, well-draining soil. They prefer a sunny, sheltered spot, and in cooler regions they do better fan-trained against a warm, protective, south-facing wall rather than on an open site. Trees may need staking and pruning to encourage branching in the first few years. Cut back the branch leaders to about half their length in winter; thereafter, you only need to prune dead or diseased wood. Mulch in the spring and water in dry spells. Pick fruit in the fall before the first frosts, when they have turned from green to golden and come away from the tree easily. Bring them into the house to ripen fully, at which point they will release their intoxicating perfume which will scent the whole house.

Apple water

This is a very good, light toner which balances oily skin. Makes approx. 8oz.

1 apple
¼ cup witch hazel
3 tablespoons cider vinegar
½ teaspoon benzoin tincture (a natural preservative)
3 drops lavender essential oil
Dark glass bottle/s

Muslin

Core the apple and discard the seeds. Chop it into small pieces and place in a pan with 1 cup of water. Bring to a boil and simmer gently for 5–10 minutes until very soft. Remove from the heat and cool.

Place a sieve over a bowl and line with muslin. Strain the apple water, then whisk in the witch hazel, vinegar, and benzoin tincture. Decant into cold, sterilized glass bottles and seal.

To use the apple water, soak a cotton pad with the mixture and wipe it gently all over the face and neck.

The water will keep for 2 weeks in the fridge.

ALTERNATIVE: QUINCE WATER

This is a particularly good toner for dry or mature skin. Make it in the same way as the apple water above, but don't core the quince. Simply chop up a quince, unpeeled, into small pieces and put it in a small pan; make sure you include the seeds. Add enough water to cover by a couple of inches. Simmer, partially covered, stirring from time to time, until the quince is very soft. Strain through a muslin-lined sieve and proceed as for the apple water. The water will keep for 2 weeks in the fridge.

GROWING APPLE AND QUINCE TREES IN POTS

If you have a small garden or patio, it's possible to grow apple and quince trees in pots, though they will need a little more attention than those grown in the ground. Choose a tree grafted onto a dwarfing rootstock. For apples, look for M27 or M9 rootstock, for quince, try a dwarfing variety which won't grow taller than 3–5ft high. Make sure you choose a self-fertile variety of apple if you only have room for one; all quinces are self-fertile. You'll need a pot around 18–24in in diameter with holes in the base for drainage. Put a layer of crocks in the bottom and then a layer of gravel to stop the soil clogging up the drainage holes. Fill the container with soil-based compost and plant the tree. Water it in well and add a layer of mulch to help the soil retain moisture. In summer, you'll need to ensure the tree is well watered, especially during hot spells, and give it a feed with a high-potash fertilizer in late winter or early spring.

Strawberry skin cream

This intensely moisturizing cream is perfect for applying to the skin after an evening bath. It contains the juice of strawberries, which are high in salicylic acid, a popular ingredient in beauty treatments because of its blemish-banishing properties. Makes approx. 14oz.

$1/2$ cup apricot kernel, jojoba, or sweet almond oil
4 tablespoons coconut or rosehip oil
2 tablespoons shea butter
1 tablespoon beeswax, grated
$5^1/2$oz ripe strawberries, hulled
$1/2$ cup rose water
$1/2$ teaspoon benzoin tincture (a natural preservative)
4 vitamin E capsules
2–3 jars

Double boiler (optional)

Place the oils, shea butter, and beeswax in a double boiler or in a bowl sitting over barely simmering water—the bottom of the bowl should not touch the water. When everything has melted together, remove from the heat and leave to cool to room temperature.

Pulse the strawberries in a food processor until very smooth. Push through a sieve to remove all of the seeds— you should have about $1/2$ cup of fine purée. Mix with the rose water and benzoin tincture. Pierce the vitamin E capsules with a pin and mix in their contents too.

Scrape the oil mixture into the processor and process for a minute at full speed. With the motor running, pour the strawberry mixture through the feed tube and process until you have a smooth and creamy emulsion—it's a little like making mayonnaise. Spoon into cold, sterilized jars and seal.

The cream will keep for 3 weeks in the fridge.

PACKAGING IDEA
Combining the cream with a beautiful bathrobe would make a perfect pampering gift.

GROWING STRAWBERRIES
Strawberries, *Fragaria*, love sunshine and rich soil, so choose a sunny spot and prepare the bed by digging in plenty of well-rotted compost. Place the plants about 16in apart, in rows which are 32in apart. When the fruits begin to appear in late spring, lay straw beneath the spreading plants to inhibit weed growth, help the soil retain moisture, and stop the fruit from lying on the ground. You may also want to throw some nets over your bed to stop the birds stealing your precious fruit. The strawberry plants' yield will start to reduce after three or four years, so replace to ensure a bountiful supply.

Toffee apples

For the perfect toffee apple, pick an apple with crisp flesh and some tartness to its flavor, to counterbalance the sweetness of the shiny toffee coating—Braeburn, Honeycrisp, Granny Smith, or McIntosh all work well. Toffee apples might be a traditional fall treat for children's parties, but don't leave them to the kids. They can also be a lighthearted, informal way to end a grown-up dinner. Makes 6.

6 apples
1/2 cup granulated sugar
1/2 cup demerara sugar
1 teaspoon cider vinegar
2 tablespoons corn syrup
2 tablespoons butter, plus a little extra for greasing

6 popsicle sticks or twigs
Candy thermometer (optional)
Cellophane and ribbon, for wrapping

Rinse the apples under very hot water, then rub them dry with a clean dish towel to remove any wax coating (which can make it difficult for the toffee to stick). Press a stick into the stalk end of each apple, making sure it's firmly secured. Line a baking sheet with parchment paper and lightly butter the parchment. If you don't have a candy thermometer, place a glass of cold water by the stove.

Place the two sugars and 3/4 cup of water in a heavy-bottomed saucepan and warm over medium-low heat until the sugar has completely dissolved. Stir in the vinegar, corn syrup, and butter. Place the candy thermometer, if you are using one, into the pan. Bring to a rolling boil and cook, without stirring, until the toffee reaches the hard-crack stage. This is when the thermometer reads 300°F, or when a small amount of mixture dropped into the glass of water will form a hard ball. This process will take 15–20 minutes, but keep a close eye on the toffee as it can burn very quickly. Remove the pan from the heat and tilt it toward you. Swirl each apple in the toffee until it's well coated and then place on the prepared baking sheet to cool.

These toffee apples, wrapped in cellophane and tied securely with ribbon, will keep well for 2–3 days in a cool, dry place.

GROWING APPLES

Even without the enormous pleasures of its versatile fruit, it would be worth growing an apple tree for its beauty alone. Wreathed in frothy blossom in spring, heavy with apples in the fall, *Malus domestica* earns its keep in any garden. There are thousands of varieties to choose from, so it's a good idea if possible to taste before you plant. If you have room for only one tree, make sure it is a self-fertile variety. If you are very short on space, investigate trees on a dwarfing or semi-dwarfing rootstock and those which can be espaliered or fan-trained against a wall. Plant bare-rooted varieties in a sunny, sheltered spot in late fall or winter, when the tree is in its dormant state. Container-grown varieties can be planted year-round, but it's best to avoid planting them in the heat of the summer to give them the best opportunity to thrive.

Roast vegetable chips

A bag of roast vegetable chips is a great gift to take to an informal party or picnic. Makes approx. 21oz.

2 beets, peeled
3 large carrots, peeled
3 large parsnips, peeled
3 tablespoons olive oil
Sea salt flakes
A few grinds of black pepper

Mandoline or sharp vegetable peeler

Preheat the oven to 400°F. Put a couple of baking sheets in the oven to warm up.

Use a mandoline or sharp vegetable peeler to pare slices of the vegetables as thinly as possible; with the carrots and parsnips, pare them in long strips. Pat the sliced vegetables with kitchen paper or a clean dish towel to remove any moisture.

Put the beets in one bowl and the carrots and parsnips in another—this stops the beets discoloring the other vegetables. Trickle some oil, salt, and pepper over the vegetables and toss them with your hands until they are thinly coated in the oil.

Remove the hot trays from the oven and quickly arrange the vegetable slices on them in a single layer (you may need to bake the chips in batches). Put them in the oven and cook for 15–20 minutes, turning them over half-way through, until the edges are crisp and they are beginning to curl. Season with a little more salt while still warm. Place the baking sheets on wire racks to cool. When the chips are completely cold, store them in an airtight container or bag.

The chips will keep in an airtight container for 3–4 days.

PACKAGING IDEA
Decorate paper bags to hold your chips with simple vegetable stamps. To create the easiest stamp of all, cut a small beet in half and hold it down firmly on a paper bag for a couple of seconds. The natural dye in the beets makes an attractive, distinctive stamp.

GROWING BEETS

Prepare your vegetable bed by making sure it's free of weeds and large stones. If possible, dig some well-rotted compost into the bed the fall before planting. Sow beet, *Beta vulgaris*, seeds directly into the ground from late spring to summer, as successive plantings every month or so will ensure a continuous supply. Sow the seeds at a depth of 1in in rows 10in apart, then rake the soil back over the seeds. Once the seeds are large enough to handle, begin thinning them out to about 4in apart. Water well during dry spells and keep the plot weed-free while the plants establish themselves. Harvest your beets when they're about the size of golf balls to enjoy them at their sweetest. One of the advantages of growing your own beets is that you get to enjoy the leaves too, which are so often lopped off when you buy them. Use the young leaves as you would spinach in salads and soups.

Spiced pear crisps

One of the great fall quests is seeking out the perfectly ripe pear. If you have lots of hard fruit, however, use them to make these spiced pear crisps. More chewy than crisp, they're a welcome present to take along on an autumnal walk. Makes approx. 50–60 crisps.

4 very firm pears
Juice of 1 lemon

4 tablespoons superfine sugar
³/₄ teaspoon ground cinnamon
¹/₂ teaspoon ground ginger
¹/₄ teaspoon grated nutmeg
Pinch of ground cloves

Mandoline
Silpat sheets or oven-proof wire racks

Preheat the oven to 250°F.

Halve each pear, remove the stem, and use a teaspoon to scoop out the core. Slice thinly using the mandoline, then place the slices in a large bowl, tossing them in the lemon juice as you go. Drain them in a colander and pat dry with paper towels or a clean dish towel. Lay the slices on a wire rack placed over a tray.

In a small bowl, combine the sugar and spices. Sift a fine dusting of the mixture over the pears, turn them over and coat the other side.

Line two large baking trays with Silpat. If you don't have Silpat sheets, place oven-proof wire racks over the baking sheets and put sheets of parchment paper on top. Place the pears on the Silpat or parchment paper and bake for about 1 hour 15 minutes, turning over once or twice. The cooking time will depend on how thin the slices are and you may need to extend it slightly. Cool the pears on wire racks. When completely cold, store in an airtight container.

The pear crisps will keep for 3–4 days.

GROWING PEARS

Give pear trees, *Pyrus communis*, a sunny, sheltered location with well-drained soil away from frost pockets. As the trees establish, water them well during dry periods, particularly once the fruit starts to swell, and mulch around the base with well-rotted compost in early spring. Some pears are self-fertile, but all fruit better with a companion. Ask the nursery about pollination groups as not all are compatible. For a small garden, consider trees on a dwarfing rootstock. Some varieties also do well as cordons, fans or espaliers.

GROWING TOMATOES

It's easy to find small tomato plants in garden centers but you will have a far wider, more interesting choice if you grow them from seed. In early spring, sow seeds in seed trays or small pots, cover them with plastic bags and place on a sunny windowsill to germinate. Transfer to 4in pots once two true leaves have formed. When the flowers on the first truss begin to open, harden them off for several days if you're going to grow them outdoors, then transfer them to 10in pots, grow bags, or plant them in the ground about 20in apart. If you're growing them in the garden rather than under glass, select a sheltered spot with as much direct sun as you can and dig some well-rotted compost into the soil a couple of weeks before you plant them out. Feed them every couple of weeks with high-potash tomato feed when they start to flower and tie cordon varieties into canes for support. Pinch out shoots that develop between the stem and main branches and water regularly and frequently to prevent the skins of the fruit splitting.

Tomato ketchup

This is a great way to make use of a glut of tomatoes. For the best flavor, it's essential that you choose very ripe fruit. Makes about 1.5 quarts.

$6^{1}/_{2}$lbs very ripe tomatoes, roughly chopped
1 onion, finely diced
$^{3}/_{4}$ cup cider vinegar
$^{1}/_{2}$ cup brown sugar
3 garlic cloves, chopped
1 teaspoon paprika
1 teaspoon salt
$^{1}/_{2}$ teaspoon English mustard powder

FOR THE PICKLING SPICES:
1 teaspoon black or white peppercorns
$^{1}/_{2}$ teaspoon allspice berries
$^{1}/_{2}$ teaspoon whole cloves
1in piece of fresh ginger, peeled and sliced
1 small bay leaf
1 blade of mace
$^{1}/_{2}$ cinnamon stick

Bottles with vinegar-proof lids
Muslin
Kitchen string
Preserving pan or large, nonreactive pan
Nylon sieve

Tie up the pickling spices in a circle of muslin with kitchen string. Put with all the other ingredients into the preserving pan. Cook over low heat until the tomatoes are pulpy and all of the sugar is dissolved, then raise the heat and simmer, stirring from time to time, for about 2 hours until the mixture has reduced and thickened. Remove the spice bag.

Place a nylon sieve over a large bowl and press the mixture through the sieve. Return it to the cleaned pan, taste, and add more sugar if necessary (the amount of sugar needed depends on how ripe and sweet the tomatoes are). Simmer the sauce for 5 minutes, or until it has the thickness you like. Decant through a funnel into hot, sterilized bottles and seal. Store in a cool, dark place for 2 weeks before using.

The ketchup will keep for 3 months, unopened, in a cool, dark place. After opening, refrigerate and use within a week.

Green tomato chutney

When the days grow shorter and an autumn chill creeps into the air, making green tomato chutney is a wonderful way to use up those tomatoes which will never ripen. For perfect texture, it's worth the effort of ensuring the vegetables are cut into even-sized chunks. Makes approx. 10 x 8oz jars.

2$\frac{1}{4}$lbs green tomatoes, diced

14oz onions, finely chopped

1 tablespoon sea salt flakes

14oz cooking apples, peeled and cored weight, diced

3 yellow bell peppers, cored and diced

3 garlic cloves, minced

1$\frac{3}{4}$ cups brown sugar

1$\frac{2}{3}$ cups cider vinegar

$\frac{1}{2}$ teaspoon red pepper flakes

FOR THE SPICE BAG

2 tablespoons of fresh ginger, peeled and sliced

1 teaspoon coriander seeds

1 teaspoon black peppercorns

1 teaspoon mustard seeds

3 cloves

1 star anise

Preserving pan or other large, nonreactive saucepan

Muslin

Kitchen string

Jars with vinegar-proof lids

Green tomatoes, because they are unripe, can take a long time to soften in cooking. Layering them beforehand in a large pan with the onions, sprinkling a little salt between each layer, and leaving overnight, will soften them and therefore shorten the cooking time.

Tie the spices into a small square of muslin with kitchen string and place in the pan with the tomatoes, onions, and all the rest of the ingredients. Stir over low heat, without boiling, until the sugar has dissolved. Bring to a boil and cook, uncovered, stirring from time to time to make sure nothing is sticking, until the chutney is thick and glossy. When you draw a wooden spoon through the middle of the pan, it should leave the bottom of the pan visible for a second or two before the mixture comes back together. This will take about 1–1$\frac{1}{2}$ hours.

Remove the spice bag and ladle the chutney into warm, sterilized jars. Seal with vinegar-proof lids and leave for at least 6 weeks before eating.

The chutney will keep in a cool, dark place for up to 2 years.

PACKAGING IDEA

A jar of this chutney with a wedge of strong, hard cheese, such as a mature Cheddar, and a box of crackers makes a great gift. Add a cheese knife too, to make it into a more substantial present.

GROWING GARLIC

Garlic, *Allium sativum*, is pleasingly uncomplicated to grow. Traditionally, it was planted on the shortest day of the year, but somewhere between the first and the last winter frost will do. Plant garlic in a sunny position, in free-draining soil. Break the bulb into cloves and plant them about 4in apart, pushing them down so the tip is about 1$\frac{1}{4}$in below the surface.

Alternatively, you can grow them in containers; about four cloves to a 6–8in pot. Keep well weeded and water well in dry periods to ensure fat, juicy bulbs. Harvest the bulbs in late summer when the leaves turn yellow. In sunny weather you can leave them hanging outside to dry; alternatively, hang them in a cool, dry, and well-ventilated place indoors. They should take about 3–4 weeks to dry fully.

Seasoned olives

Next time you're invited to a dinner party, take along a couple of jars of these seasoned olives as a tasty alternative to a bunch of flowers. Makes 2 x 18oz jars.

SEASONING FOR BLACK OLIVES
1/2 cup olive oil
6 garlic cloves, smashed
1 bay leaf
1 tablespoon finely chopped rosemary
Thinly pared zest of 1 lemon, all traces of white pith removed
12oz black olives cured in brine, rinsed

SEASONING FOR GREEN OLIVES
1/2 cup olive oil
Thinly pared zest of 1 orange
4 tablespoons finely chopped cilantro
1/2 teaspoon coriander seeds, roughly crushed in a mortar and pestle
1/4 teaspoon red pepper flakes
12oz green olives cured in brine, rinsed

2 jars

To make the black olive seasoning, pour the oil into a small pan with the garlic and warm over low heat until bubbles appear around the edge of the pan. Poach the garlic in the oil for 5 minutes, then remove from the heat. When the oil is cold, toss it with the rest of the ingredients, including the olives. Spoon into an airtight jar and refrigerate.

To make the green olive blend, simply mix all of the ingredients together, seal in a jar, and refrigerate.

The olives will keep, refrigerated, for up to 5 days. Bring to room temperature before eating.

GROWING CILANTRO

Cilantro (*Coriandrum sativum*) is a tender annual best grown in light soil where it can enjoy a little shade during the hottest part of the day. Sow it directly into the ground in late spring in 1/2in drills and cover lightly with soil. Thin out to about 4in apart once the seedlings are large enough to handle. Staggered planting throughout the summer will ensure a plentiful supply of fresh leaves. Don't overwater cilantro as it hates to be soggy, but don't let it dry out either as that will encourage its propensity to bolt. Do let some go to seed, however. Once the seeds ripen and start to become fragrant, harvest them as described on page 19.

PACKAGING IDEA If you're feeling generous, pack a pair of olive bowls into a box alongside the jars.

Zucchini & ricotta muffins

A basket of muffins is always a welcome gift. These light and tender savory ones are a delicious way of using up a plentiful crop of zucchini in summer. Alternatively, use grated carrot instead of zucchini and Cheddar in place of the Parmesan. Makes 12.

2 cups all-purpose flour
2 teaspoons baking powder
1/2 teaspoon baking soda
1/2 teaspoon salt
A few grinds of black pepper
1 teaspoon finely chopped fresh
   oregano or marjoram
1 cup Parmesan, coarsely grated
2 free-range eggs, lightly beaten
7oz ricotta
7 tablespoons olive oil
7oz zucchini, coarsely grated
5 scallions, finely chopped
Paper cases

Muffin pan

Preheat the oven to 400°F and line a muffin pan with 12 paper cases.

Sift together the flour, baking powder, and baking soda. Whisk in the salt, pepper, oregano, or marjoram and half of the Parmesan.

In a separate bowl, whisk together the eggs, ricotta, and olive oil. Fold this into the flour with a spatula until just combined—be careful not to overmix as it will make the muffins tough. Fold in the zucchini and scallions.

Spoon the batter into the paper cases and sprinkle over the rest of the Parmesan. Bake for 18–20 minutes, until a toothpick inserted into the middle of a muffin comes out clean.

These muffins are best eaten on the day of baking, though they freeze quite well.

GROWING ZUCCHINI

Zucchini, *Cucurbita pepa*, are possibly the easiest of all vegetables to grow. Sow seeds singly in small pots indoors in spring and harden them off by placing them outside in a sheltered spot during the day and then bringing them in at night for about a week. Only plant them out once all threat of frost has passed. Plant them in the ground about 3ft apart, or grow them in pots at least 16in in diameter. Keep zucchini well watered and pick them when they're no larger than 4in long for the best flavor. One of the benefits of growing your own zucchini is that you get to harvest the beautiful yellow flowers. You can eat them fresh or stuff them with soft goat cheese, dip them in a light tempura batter, and deep-fry them until golden.

Mushroom ketchup

This intensely savory condiment has been enjoyed in England for centuries, far longer than the Johnny-come-lately tomato version. It's great for adding a kick to all manner of dishes, from shepherd's pie to gravies, soups and stews. It's the secret, savory weapon in many a dedicated cook's culinary arsenal. Makes approx. 3 cups.

2½lbs mushrooms, sliced
3 tablespoons sea salt flakes
2oz dried porcini mushrooms
¾ cup red wine vinegar
4 shallots, very finely diced
2 tablespoons brown sugar

FOR THE SPICE MIXTURE
1in piece of fresh ginger, peeled
  and thinly sliced
1 small bay leaf
1 teaspoon black peppercorns
½ teaspoon allspice berries
½ teaspoon whole cloves
¼ teaspoon freshly grated nutmeg

Bottles with vinegar-proof lids

Muslin
Kitchen string
Preserving pan or large,
  nonreactive saucepan
Funnel

Layer the mushrooms in a nonreactive bowl, sprinkling salt between each layer and then on top. Cover with plastic wrap and leave in a cool place for 24 hours, stirring and pressing down on the mushrooms with a wooden spoon a couple of times as they macerate.

When you're ready to make the ketchup, put the dried porcini into a small bowl and pour over 1 cup of boiling water. Leave to soak for an hour, then scoop them out with a slotted spoon. Line a sieve with muslin and pour the soaking liquid through it into a bowl to remove any grit.

Tie the spice mixture into a circle of muslin with kitchen string.

Put the sliced mushrooms and any liquid from their bowl into the pan. Add the dried mushrooms, their soaking liquid and the rest of the ingredients, including the spice bag. Bring to a boil, lower the temperature, and simmer for about 1½ hours, stirring from time to time, until the mixture is very thick.

Remove the spice bag and blitz the mushrooms in a food processor or blender until very smooth. You may have to do this in batches. Return to the cleaned pan, bring to a boil and simmer for 5 minutes. Pour through a funnel into warm, sterilized bottles and seal. Allow to mature for a week before using.

The ketchup will keep for 3 months, unopened, in a cool, dark place. After opening, refrigerate and use within a week.

GROWING MUSHROOMS

Many people, quite rightly, are nervous about gathering wild mushrooms. If you're not absolutely sure of what you're doing, the consequences can be fatal. But by growing your own you have the pleasure of gathering mushrooms without the fear.

Mushroom-growing kits come in a wide range of varieties, from shiitake, to oyster, chestnut, hen of the woods, and portobello, to name but some of the more readily available ones. Generally, they come in two forms: plugs which you insert into holes drilled into hardwood logs or complete kits which include grow boxes and mushroom culture pre-sown with spawn. Simply follow the supplier's cultivation instructions for each variety.

PACKAGING IDEA

Growing mushrooms is a compelling hobby and one that children often enjoy too, so pack a mushroom-growing kit with the bottle of ketchup.

Onion marmalade

This marmalade is a fantastic accompaniment to cold meats, strong cheeses, and pâtés. It makes a very good Christmas present. Makes 6 x 8oz jars.

$^1/_2$ cup unsalted butter
2 tablespoons olive oil
$4^1/_2$lbs onions, halved and finely sliced
2 sprigs of thyme
1 bay leaf
1 teaspoon salt
$1^1/_4$ cups superfine sugar
1 cup cider vinegar
$^1/_2$ cup red wine
Black pepper
Jars with vinegar-proof lids

Preserving pan or large, nonreactive saucepan

Heat the butter and oil in a large saucepan over medium-low heat. When the butter stops foaming, add the onions, thyme, bay leaf, and salt. Cook gently, stirring from time to time, until the onions are very soft and a pale golden color. This will take 45 minutes to an hour. Remove the bay leaf and thyme.

Raise the heat a little, add the sugar, and continue to cook, stirring frequently, until the mixture is a deep shade of golden amber. Remove from the heat, add the vinegar, wine, and a few grinds of black pepper and give everything a good stir. Return the pan to the stove and cook fairly briskly for 30 minutes, stirring regularly, until thickened and rich.

Spoon the marmalade into warm, sterilized jars and seal with vinegar-proof lids.

The marmalade will keep for 6 months, unopened, in a cool, dark place. After opening, refrigerate and use within a week.

GROWING ONIONS

Choose a sunny, sheltered, well-drained site for your onions, *Allium cepa*, and, a few months before you want to plant them, dig the patch over, removing any stones and working in some well-rotted compost. In spring, buy immature onions, called sets, from garden centers. Plant them 4–6in apart in shallow drills and cover them so the tips are only just protruding from the soil. Keep the site as weed-free as possible and water during dry weather. Stop watering once the onions have swollen and in late summer scrape away any soil around the bulbs so they're exposed to the sun. When the foliage turns yellow, the onions are ready to harvest. Lift them and leave them to dry for a few days in the sun, or in a shed if the weather is wet.

Chile vodka

Fiery chile vodka adds a pleasing kick to a bloody mary or is delicious on its own served ice-cold in shot glasses. Makes 25oz.

2–3 hot chiles such as jalapeños, habaneros, or Hungarian hot wax, washed, plus 1–2 extra for finishing the bottle
$1/4$ teaspoon peppercorns (optional)
25oz bottle vodka

1-quart jar
25oz bottle (use the bottle the vodka came in if you like)

Funnel

Having first removed the green calyx, slice each chile in half lengthwise. Put them into a cold, sterilized 1-quart jar, with the peppercorns, if you're using them, and pour over the vodka. Seal the jar and leave in a cool, dark place for 2 weeks.

Strain the vodka into a bowl. Drop the extra chile/ies into a cold, sterilized 25oz bottle and pour the vodka in through a funnel. Seal and chill before serving.

The vodka will keep well for at least 6 months.

GROWING CHILES

Chiles are the fiery members of the capsicum family. Growing them is enormously rewarding, not just because of their myriad culinary uses but also because they make dramatically beautiful plants. Start seedlings off indoors and move them to a sunny spot outside in late spring when all threat of frost has passed.

Chiles do very well in pots, either on a sunny windowsill or on a sheltered patio. You will need to stake them when they reach about 8in and pinch out the first flowers before they set fruit in order to encourage bushy growth. Ensure that the soil doesn't dry out in hot weather, as chiles are quite thirsty, and feed them weekly after the first flowers appear with a high-potash liquid feed. Pick them as you need them, from high summer through to fall. Toward the end of the season, you can dry any which remain on the plant in a food dehydrator or in the oven on its lowest setting for around 4 hours or so.

PACKAGING IDEA

If you're feeling generous, a pretty glass pitcher and some shot glasses make a great addition to the bottle of vodka.

Chile jam

This fiery preserve goes wonderfully with strong, hard cheeses, sausages, and grilled meats. Take it along as a gift to a barbecue where not only can it be served as a condiment, but it can be also thinned with a little boiling water and used as a glaze for pieces of chicken or lamb chops. The number of chiles you use will depend on their heat and how hot you want the jam to be. Makes approx. 5 x 8oz jars.

3¹/₃lbs very ripe tomatoes, peeled and roughly chopped
4¹/₂ cups superfine sugar
1 cup red wine vinegar
2in piece of fresh ginger, peeled and grated
4–6 red chiles, halved, membranes and seeds removed and finely sliced
6 garlic cloves, finely minced
1 star anise (optional)
1 teaspoon salt
Jars with vinegar-proof lids

Preserving pan or large, non-reactive saucepan

Place all the ingredients in the preserving pan and warm over medium heat, stirring, until the sugar has dissolved. Bring to a boil, then reduce the heat and simmer, stirring from time to time, for 35–45 minutes, until the mixture has thickened and reduced to a jammy consistency. Remove the star anise.

Spoon into warm, sterilized jars and seal with vinegar-proof lids.

The jam will keep for a month, unopened, in a cool, dark place. After opening, refrigerate and use within a week.

TYPES OF CHILES TO GROW

There are so many different kinds of chiles, with different degrees of heat, it can be tricky to choose just a few. Here are some great varieties to get you started.

CHERRY BOMB MEDIUM hot and fruity, this is a great chile for sprinkling on pizza, stirring into salsas, or using in fiery pasta dishes.

HUNGARIAN HOT WAX despite its name, this is a mild- to medium-hot chile. Use it while it's mild and green or wait for it to become ripe and red if you like a little more heat. This is a very good all-around chile and one of the easiest to grow.

JALAPEÑO this chile ripens from green to red, though it is almost always used green. It's a very good chile for pickling, adding to salsas, or stuffing with cheese and roasting.

NUMEX TWILIGHT this hot chile is almost worth growing for its beauty alone. The plant displays fruits at all stages of ripeness, so it's covered in purple, yellow, orange, and red chiles all at the same time. For information on growing chiles, see page 157.

Seedy crackers

These crackers are simple to make and rival anything from an upmarket deli. The dough freezes well so make a couple of batches and keep one in the freezer for when you need to rustle up a gift at short notice. Makes approx. 30.

$1^{1}/_{2}$ cups all-purpose flour
$^{1}/_{2}$ cup spelt flour
1 teaspoon baking powder
2 tablespoons celery seeds
2 tablespoons fennel seeds
1 tablespoon caraway seeds
$^{1}/_{2}$ teaspoon freshly ground black pepper
$^{1}/_{2}$ teaspoon sea salt flakes
5 tablespoons unsalted butter, chilled and cut into small chunks

Preheat the oven to 350°F. Line two baking sheets with parchment paper.

Sift the flours and baking powder into a bowl. Whisk in the salt. Add the butter and rub in with your fingertips until the mixture resembles fine breadcrumbs. Mix in the seeds and pepper.

Make a well in the center and slowly add about $^{1}/_{2}$ cup of iced water, cutting it in with a knife to blend, then kneading it lightly with your hands until you have a firm dough. Cut the dough in half, wrap in plastic wrap, and refrigerate for 15 minutes.

Remove one piece of dough from the fridge. Place between two pieces of plastic wrap and roll out to $^{1}/_{8}$in thick. Dip a 2in round cutter in flour and cut out the crackers. Place them on the prepared baking sheet. Repeat with the other half of the dough, then refrigerate both sheets for 30 minutes.

Bake for 25–30 minutes until the crackers are just turning golden. Cool on the tray for 5 minutes, then place on a wire rack to cool completely.

The crackers will keep in an airtight container for 4–5 days.

PACKAGING IDEA

A box of these crackers with a great piece of strong Cheddar and a jar of Green Tomato Chutney (page 148) would make an excellent gift.

GROWING CELERY

Celery, *Apium graveolens*, is such an essential ingredient to so many soups and casseroles it's surprising more of us don't grow it, particularly as there are new, self-blanching varieties. Prepare the bed in a sunny spot a couple of months before you want to plant them, as for onions (page 155). Sow seeds inside in spring in seed trays or modules and cover with a fine layer of vermiculite. When large enough to handle, move them into 3in pots. Then in early summer, when the plants are about 4in high, harden them off for a few days before planting them out about 10in apart. Keep them well-watered. Harvest in late summer or early fall, though leave one or two in the ground so that you can collect the seed. Celery is a biennial. Pick the stalks when they begin to dry out and lay them out on a sheet in a warm room to finish ripening. Hold the seed heads over a bowl and break them open, collecting the seeds in the bowl. Store the seeds in an airtight jar.

Pickled walnuts

If you have a walnut tree in your garden or growing wild on public land near you, gather the green walnuts in summer to create this most traditional and delicious of treats. A jar makes a wonderful Christmas present—pickled walnuts are a great addition to the cheese board or to platters of charcuterie. Makes approx. 4$\frac{1}{2}$lbs.

4$\frac{1}{2}$lbs green walnuts
Approx. 10$\frac{1}{2}$oz salt
Large jars with vinegar-proof lids

FOR THE PICKLING MIXTURE

1 teaspoon allspice berries
$\frac{1}{2}$ cinnamon stick
$\frac{1}{2}$ teaspoon black or white
    peppercorns
1 small piece of dried ginger or
    1 tablespoon grated
    fresh ginger
1 bay leaf
1 quart white wine vinegar
1$\frac{1}{2}$ cups brown sugar

Rubber gloves
Muslin
Kitchen string
Preserving pan or large,
    nonreactive saucepan

You need to gather the immature, green walnuts before the shells have formed. Push a thin skewer or needle into the opposite end of the walnuts from the stalk and you will be able to feel if a shell is forming beneath the green outer covering. Wear rubber gloves to handle the walnuts as they stain the hands quite dramatically and stubbornly. Prick them all over with a fork or needle.

Make a brine by dissolving salt in water in a ratio of 3$\frac{1}{2}$oz salt to 1 quart water. Soak the walnuts in the brine for a week; place a plate on top to keep the nuts submerged. Drain in a colander and repeat for a further week in a fresh brine mixture.

Drain the walnuts. Place on racks lined with parchment paper in a dry, airy, and, if possible, sunny place for 2–3 days until they turn black.

Place all of the spices for the pickling mixture in a circle of muslin and tie into a bundle with kitchen string. Place the spice bundle in a large, nonreactive pan with the vinegar and sugar. Heat, stirring to dissolve the sugar, then bring to a boil. Simmer very gently for 15 minutes and discard the spice bag. Pack the walnuts into cold, sterilized jars, pour over enough of the hot spiced vinegar to cover, seal, and store in a cool, dark place for 2 months before eating.

The walnuts will keep, unopened, for up to 2 years.

PACKAGING IDEA Pickled walnuts make a good companion to strong cheeses, cured meats, and salamis, so pack up a jar in a small, luxuriously epicurean hamper.

PLANTING A WALNUT TREE

If you have the space, a walnut tree, *Juglans regia*, is a majestic addition to any garden. Plant in fall or winter in fertile, free-draining soil and provide some shelter from the wind during the early years of the tree's development, though to fruit generously it will need full sun once it becomes established. Water well during hot weather in the early years to help the tree establish, and mulch around the base of the tree to keep the soil moist. Some walnuts are partially self-fertile, but all do better if cross-pollinated, so, if possible, plant near other walnut trees.

Pickled cucumbers

If you're going to a summer barbecue, take along a jar of these sour, spicy pickles. They're the perfect condiment to add to juicy burgers. Makes approx. 2¼lbs.

2¼lbs cucumbers, sliced
1 small onion, halved and sliced
2 tablespoons sea salt flakes
1 or 2 jars with vinegar-proof lids

FOR THE PICKLING LIQUID
2 cups cider vinegar or white wine vinegar
⅓ cup superfine sugar
1 teaspoon mustard seeds
6 black peppercorns
3 allspice berries
3 garlic cloves, thinly sliced

Preserving pan or large, nonreactive saucepan

Place the cucumbers and onion in a large bowl, sprinkle over the salt, and toss with your hands. Cover and leave for 2–3 hours. Drain, rinse under the cold tap, and gently pat dry on a clean dish towel.

Put all of the ingredients for the pickling liquid into a nonreactive pan with 2 cups of water and warm gently over low heat, stirring until the sugar has dissolved. Remove from the heat and cool.

Pack the cucumbers and onions into cold, sterilized jars. Pour over the cold pickling liquid to cover completely and seal with vinegar-proof lids. Leave for 2 days for the flavors to mellow before eating.

They will keep, sealed, in the fridge for 1 month.

GROWING CUCUMBERS OUTDOORS

Cucumbers, *Cucumis sativus*, love heat but if you don't have a heated greenhouse, try varieties such as 'Gracius', 'Marketmore', and 'Burpless Tasty Green', which do quite well outdoors. Start your seeds off indoors in mid-spring in 3in pots filled with seed compost. Make a ¾in hole in the compost with a dibber/pencil and drop 2 seeds in the hole, cover with soil then water. When the seedlings are ¾in high, remove the weakest one. Harden them off for a few days before planting out in early summer in a sunny, sheltered spot, about 20in apart. Support with canes. Water in well and feed with a high-potash fertilizer once fruit starts to appear. Pick before they get too large.

Fennel & honey face mask

Fennel is a natural astringent. It cleanses the skin and reduces puffiness. In India, gram or chickpea flour is used in many natural beauty treatments as it helps draw impurities out of the skin and is a gentle exfoliant. You can buy it from Asian stores and some supermarkets.

Makes approx. 6oz, enough for 4–5 applications.

3 tablespoons fennel seeds,
  roughly crushed in a mortar and pestle
¾ cup gram or chickpea flour
4 tablespoons honey
½ teaspoon benzoin tincture
  (a natural preservative)

1 jar or pot

Place the fennel seeds in a small pan with 6 tablespoons water. Bring to a simmer and immediately remove from the heat. Let the mixture cool and infuse, then strain through a fine sieve. Whisk together with the gram flour, honey, and benzoin tincture until you have a thick paste. Spoon into the cold, sterilized jar or pot and seal.

The face mask should be smoothed onto a clean face and neck, left for 15 minutes, rubbed gently into the skin, then wiped off with a facecloth soaked in warm water. Rinse the skin in tepid water and pat dry with a fluffy towel before moisturizing.

The face mask will keep in the fridge for 2 weeks.

GROWING FENNEL

Airy fronds of fennel swaying in the breeze are such a pretty sight, and undoubtedly earn *Foeniculum vulgare* a place in the flower border, let alone the herb bed. Fennel can grow up to 5ft tall and prefers rich, well-drained soil in a sunny site, though it will tolerate less-than-perfect conditions with fairly good heart. During the summer, keep picking at the fronds to encourage lots of sweet, young leaves. *F. v.* 'Purpureum', or bronze fennel, is less vigorous and has a milder flavor but is equally beautiful. The ripening seeds take on a yellowish shade. Harvest them as described on page 19.

PACKAGING IDEA Tuck a soft, pretty facecloth into the package with the jar or pot for a simple, inexpensive but nonetheless thoughtful gift. Include a card with instructions for how to use the face mask too.

Cucumber night cream

Cucumbers are intensely hydrating and nourishing. Combined with orange blossom water and neroli oil, the essential oil of the bitter orange tree, which is believed to improve blood circulation and relieve anxiety, they make a rich night cream which relaxes as it moisturizes. Makes approx. 4 x 3½oz jars.

1 cup coconut oil
2 tablespoons white beeswax, grated
1 tablespoon shea butter
½ small cucumber, peeled, halved, seeded, and cut into chunks
4 tablespoons orange blossom water
¼ teaspoon benzoin tincture (a natural preservative)
4 drops neroli essential oil
Dark glass jars

Muslin

Place a small heatproof bowl over a pan of barely simmering water; the bottom of the bowl should not touch the water. Put the coconut oil in the bowl with the wax and shea butter. Warm, stirring from time to time, until the wax has melted. Remove the bowl from the heat and cool to room temperature.

While the oil is cooling, tip the cucumber into a blender or food processor and blitz until very smooth. Place a sieve over a bowl and line with muslin. Pass the cucumber through the sieve, pressing down with a spatula to extract as much liquid as possible. Measure 4 tablespoons of the cucumber liquid and mix with the orange blossom water, benzoin tincture and neroli oil.

Spoon the oil mixture into the cleaned food processor or blender and process for a minute. With the motor still running, pour the cucumber mixture through the feed tube and process until you have a smooth emulsion. Use a spatula to transfer the cream into cold, sterilized jars and seal.

The cream will keep in the fridge for about 10 days.

GROWING CUCUMBERS INDOORS

If you have a heated greenhouse, you can get your crop of cucumbers going sooner than those intended for outdoors. Sow seeds in early spring, as for outdoor cucumbers (page 161).

In late spring, transfer your plants to 10in pots or grow bags, two per bag. Keep the plants moist with regular watering and feed them with a diluted high-potash feed every two weeks or so. Train your cucumbers up canes or vertical wires for support. Once the main stem has reached the roof of the greenhouse, pinch out the growing point and the tips of the side shoots. Some cucumbers have male and female flowers on the same plant. With outdoor cucumbers, you can simply ignore these. With indoor ones, pinch out the male flowers as they appear. If they are left to develop, your cucumbers will be bitter. To tell male and female flowers apart, look for the swellings beneath the female flowers which will eventually become cucumbers.

Gentle lettuce cleanser

This is a very good, mild cleanser for dry or irritated skin. It's particularly soothing on sunburn, so it would make a thoughtful gift for anyone who's been a little casual with the sunscreen.

Makes approx. 13oz.

1 small, soft-leafed lettuce
1 tablespoon young borage leaves
13oz distilled water
1/4 teaspoon benzoin tincture
(a natural preservative)
2 x 7oz dark glass bottles

Muslin
Funnel

Tear the lettuce into small pieces and place in a pan with the borage and distilled water. Bring to a boil, immediately lower the temperature and simmer very gently, partially covered, for 30 minutes. Remove from the heat and cool. Line a sieve with muslin and strain the liquid into a bowl. Whisk in the benzoin tincture. Decant into cold, sterilized bottles and seal.

The cleanser will keep for 2 weeks in the fridge.

GROWING LETTUCE

What could be simpler to grow, and more delicious, than your own lettuce? With a little planning, you can have fresh leaves for most months of the year. Sow *Lactuca sativa* seeds every couple of weeks from spring until late summer to ensure a continuous supply. Plant the seeds about 1/2in deep in fertile, well-drained soil in a spot where they'll have some shade from the midday sun. Thin out seedlings once the first true leaves appear so that they're about 12in apart. Of course, you can add the thinnings to salads, so nothing is wasted. Loose-leaf varieties are among the least demanding types to grow, which is fortunate as not only are they delicious, but they're also the sort of lettuce you need to make this cleanser. Cut-and-come again varieties also grow very well in containers. All lettuce likes water, so be careful not to let the soil dry out.

Creamed horseradish

Creamed horseradish goes beautifully, of course, with roast beef and so makes a great homemade gift to take along to a Sunday lunch. Makes 2 x 5½oz jars.

3½oz crème fraîche
3½oz heavy cream, lightly whipped
3½oz fresh horseradish root,
   finely grated
Pinch of sugar
Salt and freshly ground white pepper
   2 jars

Gently fold together the crème fraîche and cream until well combined. Stir in the horseradish and sugar and season to taste with salt and pepper.

Seal in cold, sterilized jars and refrigerate until ready to use.

Creamed horseradish will keep, refrigerated, for 2 days.

GROWING HORSERADISH

In many regions, horseradish, *Amoracia rusticana*, grows in abundance along the roadside, but make sure you get permission from the landowner before you dig it up. It is, however, very easy to grow your own. Some may say too easy: horseradish is an invasive perennial, so be careful where you place your plant. It will tolerate all kinds of soils but doesn't like heavy shade, so choose a sunny spot. In spring, take a live root about 10in long and plant it in a hole at a depth of about 6in, allowing about 18in between plants. To contain its growth, horseradish can also be grown in planters such as half-barrels.

Lift horseradish roots as you need them in the fall. To store roots over the winter, when the ground is too cold to dig them up, lift a few roots and store them in a cool, dark place in a box of dry sand.

PACKAGING IDEA

Combined with a jar of Pickled Cucumbers (page 161) or Green Tomato Chutney (page 148), either of these preserves make a great addition to a savory gift basket.

Pickled horseradish

Slivers of pickled horseradish add a fiery bite to many dishes, with a flavor reminiscent of Chinese pickled ginger. They can be eaten as an accompaniment to mackerel, smoked salmon, or strong, hard cheeses. Makes 2 x 8oz jars.

14oz fresh horseradish root, peeled
   and thinly sliced with a sharp knife
   or mandoline
2 tablespoons sea salt flakes
¾ cup rice vinegar or cider vinegar
3 tablespoons superfine sugar
Juice and finely grated zest of 1 lime
Juice and finely grated zest of 1 lemon
Juice and finely grated zest of
   ½ small orange
2 jars with vinegar-proof lids

**Preserving pan or large,
   nonreactive saucepan**

Place the horseradish in a bowl with the salt and stir to combine. Cover and leave for 12 hours or overnight, stirring once or twice. Place the horseradish in a colander and rinse briefly under cold water. Leave to drain for 15 minutes, then pat dry with a clean dish towel.

Warm the vinegar, sugar, and ½ cup of water in a pan until simmering, stirring to dissolve the sugar. Add the lime, lemon, and orange juices and zests and remove from the heat immediately.

Divide the horseradish between the two sterilized jars and pour the vinegar mixture over to cover. Seal, cool, and refrigerate for a minimum of 7 days for the flavors to develop.

Refrigerated, this will keep for 1 month.

Carrot cake

Next time you're asked to bring along a cake to a party, try this moist carrot cake fragrant with spices and covered with tangy cream cheese icing.

Makes 9 squares or 1 round 9in cake.

1 cooking apple, about $1/2$lb, peeled, cored, and diced

Grated zest and juice of 1 small orange

$3/4$ cup raisins or golden raisins

$1^2/3$ cups self-rising flour

2 teaspoons baking powder

1 teaspoon ground cinnamon

1 teaspoon ground ginger

$1/2$ teaspoon grated nutmeg

$1/2$ teaspoon salt

$2/3$ cup butter, melted, plus extra for greasing

3 free-range eggs

$2/3$ cup brown sugar

9oz carrots, peeled and coarsely grated

3oz pecans or walnuts, toasted and roughly chopped, plus 9 whole ones to decorate

FOR THE ICING

4 tablespoons unsalted butter, at room temperature

9oz cream cheese, at room temperature

1 teaspoon lemon juice

Finely grated zest of 1 small lemon

$2^1/3$ cups confectioners' sugar, sifted

8 x 8 x 3in square cake pan or a 9in loose-bottomed cake pan

Preheat the oven to 325°F. Grease the cake pan and line the bottom and sides with parchment paper. Butter the parchment.

Put the apple into a small pan with the orange juice and the raisins. Cook gently until the apples are soft and pulpy. Leave to cool.

Sift together the flour, baking powder, cinnamon, ginger, nutmeg, and salt.

In a separate bowl, whisk together the butter, eggs, and sugar until they are very light and foamy. Gently fold in the flour until just combined, then fold in the apple sauce, orange zest, carrots, and chopped nuts. Spoon into the prepared pan and bake for 50 minutes to an hour, until a toothpick inserted into the middle comes out clean. Cool in the pan for 10 minutes before turning out the cake to cool completely on a wire rack.

To prepare the icing, beat the butter until fluffy, then gradually beat in the cream cheese until you have a smooth mixture with no lumps. Beat in the lemon juice and zest. Gradually beat in the confectioners' sugar.

When the cake is completely cold, ice and decorate with the remaining whole nuts.

The cake will keep in an airtight container, uniced for 3–4 days. It's best iced just before you intend it to be eaten.

GRoWING CARRoTS

Carrots love light, sandy soil with a fine, crumbly texture so they can develop into nice, straight roots. Sow the seeds directly in the soil from spring through to early summer. Early sowings may need some protection with cloches or horticultural fleece. Successive plantings every few weeks will give you a continuous supply. Sow where you want them to grow as thinning can release chemicals which attract hungry carrot flies. You can deter them by planting some chives (page 23) nearby. Sow carrot seeds very thinly—if you find this difficult, mix the tiny seeds with some sharp sand to make them easier to handle—and cover with a fine layer of soil. Aim to plant them about $1/2$in deep in rows 5in apart. Don't let the soil dry out and keep the patch well weeded. Your first carrots should be ready to lift about 8 weeks later.

Hazelnut praline

Clear as amber glass and studded with toasted hazelnuts, this praline is heavenly to nibble on or, chopped or crushed into small pieces, as a delicious decoration for ice cream or cakes. Makes 1 sheet of praline.

5¹/₂oz whole unblanched hazelnuts
³/₄ cup granulated sugar
¹/₂ teaspoon sea salt flakes (optional)
A little vegetable oil, for greasing

12 x 12in baking sheet
Silpat mat (optional)

Preheat the oven to 400°F. Place the hazelnuts on a high-sided baking sheet and bake until they are fragrant and the skins are blistered, about 5 minutes. Wrap them in a clean dish towel and leave for 5 minutes before rubbing vigorously to remove the skins—don't worry too much if some of the skins remain on the nuts.

Next, make the praline. Assemble everything before you start. Lightly oil the baking sheet or line it with a Silpat mat if you have one.

Put the sugar into a heavy-bottomed saucepan or frying pan. It's better to use a pan that has a pale interior, rather than a dark one, in order to monitor the color of the caramel more easily. Warm the sugar over medium heat. It will begin to melt. At this stage, stir it slightly to encourage it to melt evenly. Lower the heat a little and leave to melt completely without stirring until the caramel is a rich, golden brown. Don't leave it unattended even for a moment; it can burn very quickly. As soon as it's ready, add the hazelnuts and turn out onto the prepared baking sheet, swirling to ensure it's a thin, even layer. Sprinkle over the sea salt, if using. Leave to set and cool for an hour or so before breaking into pieces.

The praline will keep, sealed in an airtight container, for 2 weeks.

GROWING HAZELNUTS

'Hazel' is the common name for a species of nut-bearing shrub which includes the cobnut, *Corylus avellana*, and the filbert, *C. maxima*.

Though hazels are theoretically self-fertile, bearing golden male catkins and small, red female flowers on the same bush, often their flowering times don't overlap. As they're wind-pollinated, unless you live in the countryside where there are many wild hazels, you need to plant a mixture of varieties to ensure a good crop. Hazels grow best in well-drained soil in a sunny position, but they will also tolerate a little shade. Young bushes and trees should start to be productive after three or four years—the nuts are ready to harvest when the husks begin to turn yellow in the fall.

PACKAGING Praline makes a great gift for an ice-cream fiend. Seal in a pretty, airtight container alongside an ice-cream scoop and some sundae glasses.

SUPPLIERS

MICHAEL'S

A large craft superstore, with supplies for all types of projects and crafts. Stores are located across the country.
www.michaels.com

BURPEE

Specialty seed store, with a large online selection of seeds for fruit, vegetables, flowers, perennials, and herbs. Burpee also sells a line of organic seeds. The site also features seed starting supplies, as well as general gardening supplies.
www.burpee.com

GURNEY'S SEED & NURSERY CO.

A comprehensive seed store, with a large online selection of seeds for fruit, vegetables, flowers, perennials, and herbs.
P.O. Box 4178
Greendale, IN
47025-4178
513-354-1491
www.gurneys.com

THE NATURAL GARDENING COMPANY

The oldest certified organic nursery in the United States. The Natural Gardening Company specializes in certified organic plants (vegetable, herb, and flower seedlings), certified organic seeds, and drip irrigation supplies.
P.O. Box 750776
Petaluma CA
94975-0776
707-766-9303
www.naturalgardening.com

JAMALI GARDEN

An excellent source of interesting containers and vases for floral arrangements sourced from around the world, as well as general floral supplies. There is a retail store in New York City.
Jamali Garden
149 West 28th Street (Between 6th and 7th Avenue)
212-244-4025
212-996-5534
www.jamaligarden.com

WILLIAMS-SONOMA

A cooking and housewares store, including gardening supplies. The store features high-quality and specialized items for cooking and entertaining, as well as a gourmet food and drink selection.
www.williams-sonoma.com

PEACEFUL VALLEY FARM AND GARDEN SUPPLY

A family owned company based in California that specializes in organic gardening supplies and seeds. All seeds are certified GMO free. The Grass Valley, CA store and nursery specializes in California natives and ornamental edibles. They also have a large selection of products available online.
Retail Location:
Peaceful Valley Farm & Garden Supply
125 Clydesdale Court
Grass Valley, CA 95945
To place an order, call toll free at 1-888-784-1722
To ask questions call 530-272-4769
www.groworganic.com

GARDENER'S SUPPLY COMPANY

Online gardening superstore, feature a wide range of gardening supplies, including seed starting kits, soil and potting mixes, pots and planters, gardening tools, composting materials, landscaping items such as trellises and arches and arbors, and watering supplies.
www.gardeners.com
1-888-833-1412

BULK APOTHECARY

A soap and candle-making online store with a variety of supplies, it also features a range of essential oils and lip balm-making supplies.
1800 Miller Parkway
Streetsboro, Ohio
44241
1-888-968-7220
www.bulkapothecary.com

NASHVILLE WRAPS

A company that carries a wide range of gift wrap supplies, from wrapping paper to gift bags and boxes to food packaging to candy boxes and more. It also features a range of eco-friendly gift and food packaging materials.
242 Molly Walton Drive
Hendersonville, TN
37075
1-800-547-9727
www.nashvillewraps.com

HOBBY LOBBY

A craft superstore, with supplies for all types of projects and crafts, as well as seasonal supplies. Stores are located across the country.
www.hobbylobby.com

PAPER SOURCE

Paper Source sells acid-free glassine envelopes in small batches, particularly useful when some online suppliers only sell them by the thousand. Perfect for storing seeds and dried flowers, and for a wide range of other craft projects. This store offers a wide range of paper products, along with additional craft supplies. Paper Source has both an online store and retail stores located across the country.
www.paper-source.com

INDEX